RULES

OF THE

CONGREGATION OF THE HOLY CROSS.

NOTRE DAME, IND.:

AVE MARIA PRESS.

1871.

INTRODUCTION.

The following Rules may well be considered the fruit of experience—the most important of all schools—as well as the result of long meditations and the promptings of a heart profoundly impressed with the gravity of the task, and no less with the desire to secure by them the success of the Congregation with the happiness and sanctification of all its members.

But it may be equally well to declare at once, and once for all, that even if a greater care could have been bestowed upon them—if they were in truth the best Rules by which a Community could be governed—still they would avail but little, and obtain no satisfactory result, either for the Congregation as a body or for its individual members, unless they be received and studied and acted upon with a special disposition, which alone can give them some virtue, and such a virtue as to procure the sanctification of each and every Religious in the family, and the highest respectability of the

Order in the estimation of the world. What is this precious disposition? Is it found in the fact of having brought to the Community a fortune, an accomplished education, a rare talent, or any other temporal advantage? No; in none of these. It is something far more valuable, while it is within the reach of all. It is simply this: the spirit of faith; of "that faith without which it is impossible to please God". It is that mysterious disposition which reveals God's holy will to the eyes and to the heart of a Religious, and makes every line of his Rules a source of contentment and merit; it is that holy spirit which transforms, in a Community truly deserving of the name, exercises, duties, labors, and fatigues, into as many manifestations of Divine love; every act of obedience to superiors into a homage to God Himself; which, in reality, ennobles every act even of a poor, illiterate, unnoticed, and yet devoted, Religious, whose constant attention to God's holy presence and whose humble prayers save the House where he lives, while by it he becomes a living edification to all, and an object of admiration to the angels themselves.

The spirit of faith sustains him in the hour of

trial, of affliction and sickness; for, in the light of faith, the tribulations of this life can bear no comparison with the weight of glory awaiting his patience in eternity.

Oh! the blindness of human judgments! Here is a modest Religious, unheeded and ignored by the world; or pitied by the world as one blindly running to a state of slavery, or foolishly preferring a forlorn condition to the enjoyment of liberty and of all the comforts of life; and yet this voluntary slave feels happier in the folly of the Cross than the world could ever make him. One day, by a ray of the light of Divine faith, he clearly saw—he felt, he realized—the emptiness of worldly joys, and the cruel bitterness of its deceptions. Beneath its flowery path and its glittering promises he discovered by the same ray the snares, the perils, the enemies in wait for his immortal soul. He paused in prayer. The Cross, the naked Cross upon which man's salvation was consummated, rose up to the eyes of his mind; a secret virtue drew the aspirations of his heart towards the Divine Emblem on which he read a promise of eternal life. In the generosity of his soul he resolved to leave all, and range himself among the soldiers of the Cross. From that hour "he found not where his foot could rest" in the world, until he retired from it and entered the ark of safety. From that hour all his ambition was to live for Him who had died on the Cross for love of him.

Now he lives for Him, and for Him exclusively: "Far be it from him to glory in anything but in the Cross of Christ our Lord." "For he knows whom he has believed," that he "has chosen the best part," and that if he "persevere to the end he shall be saved." Hence his attention in all his duties, and in whatever he does, to do all in a spirit of faith to honor the Divine Master in the mystery of the Cross.

The Religious of the Holy Cross should ever glory, like St. Paul, in their glorious Standard, and carry it high above all terrestrial passions and sentiments. They may never be called to shed their blood for Him who redeemed us on the Cross, but they should love the Cross none the less, and never feel either ashamed or afraid of the Cross.

There is sometimes a great deal in a name: is not ours a beautiful and a suggestive one? By itself it reveals, even to the humblest among us, the characteristic features of our peculiar vocation. We are declared by our very name the soldiers, the lovers of the Cross. It is in this light of faith we must see and estimate our duties, and receive a direction to fulfil them meritoriously.

Such is the aim of the present volume of the Rules, revised with due care, and, we trust, made practicable in all points.

We commend their faithful observance to each and to all of our Religious, by all that we and they hold most sacred; upon this fidelity rests the destiny of our Congregation. A loose Community is a scandal; but a Community living up to its Rules is a blessing among men, a power in the Church for the struggle in which she is engaged, and an honest pride for its fervent members.

May they be blessed from above, and prove a source of blessings to our dear Congregation. We ask no other reward for our pains.

E. S.

Feast of the Presentation, 1871.

RULE I.

Of the End of the Congregation.

Be ye perfect, as your Heavenly Father is perfect.
—*St. Matt.*, v, 48.

The end of this Congregation is, in common with all Religious Orders, the sanctification of its members by a constant application to the acquisition of all virtues; and also the salvation of souls, after the example of Jesus Christ, who began to do and then to teach: or, in other words, the first end of the Congregation is to sanctify its members through a life of perfection; while the second is to assist the Church in the salvation of souls, by means of preaching and teaching.

Although composed of two distinct elements, Ecclesiastics and Laymen—the former consecrated to the Sacred Heart of Jesus, under the name of Salvatorists, and the latter dedicated to the glorious spouse of Mary, St. Joseph, under that of Josephites—all its members are blended together under the same designation of Religious of the Holy Cross, with the same vows and obligations, and the same interests, with a training proper to each. There is no other distinction between them than that which is dictated by faith, and so carefully and solemnly kept in view by our Holy Church.

The Fathers and the Brothers of the Holy Cross have been constituted together, by the Holy See, into a new Religious Family, that by their united efforts they may the better secure what is most needed in our age. In this union the Church has anticipated and welcomed the double guarantee of usefulness and efficiency. No man should ever separate, even in thought, what God's Vicar on earth has joined to remain one in devotedness to the same holy cause.

The special end of the Fathers is to preach Retreats and Missions, and to teach Theology and Philosophy, and other Ecclesiastical Sciences, with classical and scientific branches in universities and colleges. That of the Brothers is to assist as teachers and prefects in colleges; to conduct parochial schools (to which, whenever it is practicable, they annex boarding-schools); to take charge of orphan asylums and industrial schools; and, finally, to devote themselves to the various departments of manual labor attendant upon colleges, farms, &c.

In proportion as they strive in earnest to reach their first and common end,—viz., their personal sanctification—the former by a close imitation of the dispositions of the Sacred Heart, and the latter by faithfully reproducing the humble, meritorious life of St. Joseph,—experience shows that they succeed in obtaining their second and particular one, either in the pulpit or the class-room, in the field, the workshop, &c., &c.

RULE II.

Of the Means to Reach the End.

The first end of the Congregation, viz., the sanctification of its members, is obtained by a regular series of religious exercises and practices for each day, as Meditation, Holy Mass, Particular Examen, Spiritual Reading, Beads, and Visit to the Blessed Sacrament; for each week, as Confession, Communions, Chapter, and Adoration; for every month, as Monthly Retreat, Direction, and Monition; and annually, the General Retreat.

Besides this, a considerable assistance is found daily and hourly in the community life led by its members, in the edifying examples of a pious and well-regulated family, in the continual and paternal watchfulness of Superiors, and in the faithful observance of the three vows under which all have chosen to live.

The secondary and particular end is reached in

both branches by a special and thorough training—viz., for the Priests, by a regular classical course, and a serious study of philosophy, dogmatic and moral theology, of Holy Scriptures, &c., all of which require conscientious quarterly examinations; and for the Brothers by a proper course of studies in all elementary branches taught in the public schools of the land. Not only are they taught all the branches necessary to enable them to sustain successfully the competition of other schools, but they have to learn and practise, before being sent out on mission, the plan of studies and method of conducting schools of which the Congregation has charge.

Above all, the great, the special means to secure the end of the Congregation is to seek the Kingdom of God, and live by faith; and next to this spiritual means comes in point of importance the following measure, dictated by human wisdom and supported by sober reason and common sense, viz.: to commence from the Novitiate to unite in the bonds of respect and love all Religious destined to live together for life, blended together by apostolic sanction as a condition of Religious acknowledgment in the Church; not that they should permit the friendly intercourse of daily life to degenerate into familiarity and want of respect; but the Brothers should learn how they, as laymen, should look upon the anointed of God, and those who prepare themselves to be pastors of souls and the vicegerents of Christ should reproduce towards their Brothers the benignity, the meekness and charity of their Divine Model. If all are led by faith, the foundation of a happy and useful life cannot fail to be laid in the common Novitiate.

Last, but not least, among the means by which the Congregation reaches its end is the name each member gives it before the public by his conduct and his virtues, by his piety and devotedness to its interests, and by the services he renders it. Thus each member becomes a means to strengthen, elevate and extend the Congregation.

Here is the question which every Religious should ask himself at times: Am I a help to the Community? or am I not a burden, a hindrance in it—a cross to my Superiors, a disedification to my associates? Let all bear in mind that whatever gift God has bestowed upon them, whether brain or muscle, talent or ability of any sort, was intended as a means to uphold the Congregation, to be consecrated to its service in order to enable it to accomplish its end and to fulfil Heaven's designs.

RULE III.

Of Admission to the Postulate.

Pray ye therefore the Lord of the harvest that He send forth laborers into His vineyard.—*St. Matt.* ix, 38.

In the above sacred text every true Religious finds the expression of one of the inmost wishes of his soul; for, as experience clearly shows, a true Religious is ever anxious for the increase and development of his Congregation. This is his abiding desire; and in proportion as he values his own vocation and loves his Community he prays for new accessions; and in answer to his fervent zeal God frequently gives him grace to awaken in young hearts aspirations analogous to his own. A bad Religious destroys around him all such resolutions; but a good and exemplary one encourages and happily brings them to maturity: here, emphatically, both are known by their fruit.

A choice, however, has to be made; and to prevent deception or imposition, the following method shall be followed respecting applications from strangers not personally known by any member of the Community. When such a request for admission is received, a printed series of questions, as the following, is sent in reply:

State your name and surname; those of your father and mother; your age; the place of your birth; that of your residence; your profession or employment; the profession of your parents; your constitution and health; your natural dispositions; your proficiency in point of education; where you acquired it; how long you pursued your studies. Were you born and baptized in the true faith? Have you your certificate of baptism, and what recommendations can you bring? Were you ever married, or bound by a promise of marriage? Were you ever a member of some other Community? Are you not necessary to your parents, or charged with any other responsibility or debts or obligations to anybody? Is your character blameless, and has it always been so? Are you entirely free from any hereditary or contagious disease? Do you feel sincerely disposed to bind yourself to a life of poverty, obedience and chastity? Are you willing to be tried by a regular novitiate, without any dispensation from any Rule of the Order? Can you depend upon the firmness of your determination to save your soul in Religion? Have you means to defray the expenses of your novitiate? Can you bring an outfit of clothes sufficient for at least one year? Do you come to be a teacher, or to place yourself unreservedly in the hands of your Superiors?

When conscientious and honest answers shall have been affixed to the foregoing queries, singly and separately, with proper date and signature, the sheet thus duly filled shall be sent back to the Secretary or Superior. If satisfactory to the Provincial Council (or Special Committee), the applicant is received, and an invitation to come is immediately forwarded.

When the candidate arrives he is presented to the Very Rev. Father Provincial, by whom he is introduced to the Master of Novices.

If the candidate be a Priest, a room is given him, through respect for his sacred character; if he be a candidate for Holy Orders, he is placed in a room with one or more of the same class; the postulants for the Brothers sleep in a common dormitory.

Two days are given to newly arrived postulants to prepare themselves for a general confession, or a review of life covering an epoch of at least the last few years.

Then an exact inventory is taken, in the Book of Novices, of whatever they bring with them. This is signed by themselves. They deposit their money in the treasury.

On another sheet of printed form they obligate themselves, in case they should leave or be found without a vocation, to pay for their board and other expenses whilst in the Novitiate, if they had studied, and that they shall never ask any remuneration for work or services performed since their entrance.

They are immediately admitted to the exercises of the Novitiate, where they remain as candidates, under the especial care of the Assistant Master of Novices, until their dispositions are fully known and a moral certainty is obtained of their fitness for the Congregation, or until they are of a proper age to receive the Religious habit—viz., 15 years.

Prudence requires that candidates be thoroughly examined, and tried for a considerable time rather than be exposed to leave after a hasty admission. In case of doubt, no action can be taken until time has removed it.

Postulants are dismissed for the following reasons, namely: 1. The discovery of any of the impediments mentioned in Constitution V, Art. 29. 2. Any attempt against pure morals. 3. A fault-finding spirit; a habitual disposition to complain or criticise or murmur. 4. Repeated irregularity in attending exercises and duties, especially in rising at the first signal; or want of zeal for discipline or piety. 5. A spirit of haughtiness or independence, or no inclination to Religious obedience. 6. A sickly constitution, a diseased mind, an unsound judgment, an eccentric disposition that can do nothing like the rest. 7. A lack of regard for Rules, Superiors, and authority in general.

When any one of the above has been ascertained, and made known to the postulant, without producing amendment, the same is reported to the Provincial, who pronounces his dismissal, unless in his prudence and for some particular reason he deem it expedient to have recourse to some new means, and protract his trial a while longer.

RULE IV.

Of the Admission to the Novitiate, and of its Exercises.

The word "novitiate" signifies either a place or a time or a certain manner of living. As a place, it means a retired spot where the soul, delivered from the noise and bustle, as well as from the cares and anxieties, of the world, may enjoy a little rest in silent and undisturbed communion with God. As a time, it is one year at least, or two at most, spent thus, as it were, away from the gaze of the world—not in idleness, but in a new kind of life, which forms the third meaning of the word, and the most important and comprehensive of the three. By it we understand a serious and conscientious examen of one's self, leading in the end to a thorough knowledge of self; a progressive transformation into a new being; the laying of a broad foundation for a noble structure; a special training for a special end, by special means. Such is the nature or object of the Novitiate.

To succeed in making a good Novitiate, on which evidently depends the success of a whole life, one must be willing to be formed—shaped and moulded, in a manner—by the hands of the Master of Novices. Hence the necessity of obedience and simplicity on the part of those who wish to become efficient and edifying members of the Congregation. The means by which such an important result is secured are easy, and within the reach of all who have a good will; but a good and earnest will is indispensable.

The training of Novices consists in the following exercises and practices:

Every day: half an hour of Meditation in common in the morning; Holy Mass, immediately after Meditation, at 6 o'clock; the Breviary or Little Office at 7.30; Explanation of the Christian Doctrine, and Particular Examen, from 11.30 to 12; Vespers at 1.30, Matins and Lauds at 4; Explanation of the Directory, and Visit to the Blessed Sacrament, from 6 to 6.30; at 8 o'clock—Beads, Spiritual Reading, Evening Prayer, and Points of Meditation for the following morning.

Every week: One hour of Adoration, in common; Friday, Chapter—at 3 o'clock for the Priests, and at 8 for the Brothers—and the Way of the Cross; Saturday, Confession in the morning, and the Litany of Loretto in the evening.

Every month: A Monthly Retreat, Direction, and Monition.

Studies and classes daily from 8 until 10, and from 10.30 until 11.30, in the forenoon; from 2 until 4, and from 5 until 6 in the afternoon.

If required, the Novices may teach one or two hours a day in the College, if there is one close by; the Ecclesiastics may also follow the courses of philosophy and theology there. But whether they teach or be taught, the Novices shall go and return together, in silence, and remain in the College only for their classes.

On Wednesday afternoons the Master of Novices takes a walk with the Ecclesiastic Novices and Postulants; his Assistant accompanies the others. The object of the former should be to visit the sick or to instruct such poor and ignorant families as may be in the vicinity, as a preparation for their future mission.

The studies and classes are left to the direction of the Master of Novices. There is, for all, a quarterly examination in all the branches taught in the Novitiate, before the members of the Provincial Council, and notes are given under the following headings, namely: Health, aptitude, regularity conduct, temper, Directory, Rules, Chant, progress in studies.

The Novices not intended for study recite, instead of the Little Office, seven *Pater*, *Ave*, and *Gloria*, three times a day—namely, after Mass; at 1 p. m.; and after supper; in the chapel or wherever duty has called them.

All meals are taken in silence. At breakfast the *Following of Christ* is read; at dinner, a portion of the Gospel (from ten to fifteen verses), then the *History of the Church* and the *Martyrology;* at supper, the Life of a Saint and three paragraphs of the *Rules*.

For the rest, namely the ringing of the bell, the sweeping and cleaning of the corridors and rooms, the care of the chapel, of the refectory, &c., all is left to the Master of Novices to arrange as he may deem fit and proper.

On Sunday and Wednesday there is one hour devoted to the practice of singing and church ceremonies.

All the exercises of the Novitiate are performed in common, except the Chapter on Friday.

The Catechetical Instruction at 11.30 is given by one of the Ecclesiastics in turn, by way of preparation. In the same manner the subject of Meditation is given out by one of them on Saturday night.

Rodriguez and St. Jure should be read alternately at Spiritual Reading.

The same reasons which necessitate the dismissal of a Postulant apply likewise to that of a Novice, with only this difference, that the latter case being so much more deplorable, the Provincial lays it before his Council previous to final action. In either case, great charity is used towards the unfortunate subject, who is not unfrequently so blinded as not yet to realize the misery he has brought upon himself.

RULE V.

Of Prayer and Meditation.

We ought always to pray, and not to faint.—*St. Luke*, xviii, 1.

Prayer is an elevation of the soul to God. It is the food of the soul, as bread is the food of the body.

There are two kinds of prayer: vocal, or uttered by the lips; and mental, or that which passes in the mind and produces affections in the heart. The latter, or meditation, communicates to the soul that abiding spirit of prayer so highly recommended by the Saviour, and which forms a constant elevation towards God by frequent aspirations from the heart, by an incessant and loving attention to God's holy presence, and by a purity of intention continually renewed throughout the various actions of the day.

Both are excellent, but as they have already been fully explained in the *Directory* we say no more here on the subject, except that whenever a Religious of the Holy Cross betakes himself to prayer, he ought to pray well or not at all.

The Cross being our special and glorious standard, no one among the members of the Congregation should attempt to bless himself with its saving sign without that due reverence by which indeed every member of the Community should be known everywhere.

To secure recollection in prayer, imagine that you kneel at the foot of the Cross on Mount Calvary, and, after a pause, sign yourself, slowly, religiously, piously—and not hurriedly and scandalously.

The importance attached to the sign of the Cross is more serious than is imagined by many. From time to time, the Religious of the Holy Cross should make it the subject of their Particular Examen, and see how they honor the Sacred Standard under which they have volunteered to fight and to die. All must have the same, uniform manner of making the sign of the Cross, viz.: placing the hand on the forehead while saying "In the name of the Father," lowering it to the breast while saying "and of the Son," then crossing from the left to the right shoulder while saying "and of the Holy Ghost," and concluding with "Amen" as the hand is coming down again.

Whenever the Community is assembled in prayer complete silence must be observed; no noise whatever is allowed, either in walking, rising, coughing, &c., for fear of disturbing anyone. Whether kneeling or sitting, a respectful and reverential posture must always be taken at prayer.

RULE VI.

Of the Divine Office, and of the Little Office.

Seven times a day I have given praise to Thee.
—*Ps.* cviii, 164.

In order to offer to God the sacrifice of praise spoken of by the royal prophet, the Novices recite at stated hours the Divine Office or the Little Office of the Blessed Virgin—the Ecclesiastics in Sacred Orders together, and the Brothers by themselves.

Ecclesiastics and Brothers shall endeavor to discharge with attention and piety this liturgical duty, which, after the Eucharistic Sacrifice, may prove the most abundant source of blessings both for themselves and the whole Congregation. True Religious always feel honored and delighted in being thus permitted to join with the Blessed Spirits above in the praises of God. This being the prayer of the Church, and of the purest of her children, attention shall be paid to pronounce every word of it distinctly and piously, neither too fast nor too slow, but in perfect accord and unison of all the voices. So much for Novices at the Novitiate. Once acquired, the habit of reciting the Divine Office or the Little Office well must be preserved for life.

The teaching Brothers shall recite it in common in each establishment, and will find it everywhere a rich source of consolations and graces.

Each Ecclesiastic recites it generally by himself. The most fervent among them always say their Office at the first moment permitted by the rubrics, while the less regular postpone it to the last hours of the day, when their mind is wearied and they are half sleepy. Proper time and place and position should be taken to discharge this important duty.

RULE VII.

Of Holy Mass and Communion.

Do this in commemoration of Me.—*St. Luke*, xxii, 19.

Here again we refer to the *Directory*, in which the same subjects are treated of at length, with appropriate prayers for preparation and for thanksgiving.

Such should be the holiness of a Priest's life, even in the world, as to permit him daily to ascend the altar; and such is, indeed, the general practice among pious priests everywhere. With greater reason is the same piety looked for in a Religious Priest.

The Priests of the Congregation shall celebrate at the altar and at the hour assigned them, and for the intentions handed them monthly, with the exception of five days each month, the disposition of which is left to themselves.

No one is at liberty to go and celebrate outside of the premises, without a special leave or appointment. All honoraries or stipends received for Masses must be handed in full to the Secretary.

Unless Mass be celebrated immediately after Meditation or the Divine Office, a preparation for it is made during at least ten minutes: and a thanksgiving after Mass for fifteen minutes or more.

As much as possible, the Superiors shall officiate on solemn festivals and on the feasts of the Patron Saints of the Congregation. At low Masses celebrated by the Superior General, the Provincials in their Province, or the Visitors in their official visits, two Ecclesiastics in cotta, or two Brothers with the Roman cloak, shall serve, and four candles shall be lighted on the altar instead of two. In boarding-schools it is edifying to see the students serve Mass daily.

The Ecclesiastic Novices and Scholastics attend Holy Mass every day, and receive Holy Communion oftener as they approach nearer the time of their ordination. If any act upon earth require attention, recollection and piety, undoubtedly it is the Holy Sacrifice of Mass. A saint relates that whenever St. John Chrysostom celebrated Mass, crowds of angels descended from heaven, and that the Saint usually saw them clothed in white, with feet bare, prostrating themselves before the altar with profound respect till the end of the Holy Sacrifice.

A Priest does wrong if he fail to offer this Divine Sacrifice, because he deprives the Holy Trinity of infinite praise and glory, our Lord of great joys, the blessed of new delights, the souls in purgatory of relief in their sufferings, and himself of very great advantages.

It is true that the Priest alone offers the sacrifice of the Mass to God; but it is equally true that all the faithful who attend it are invited to join with him in spirit and offer it with him; for the minister represents the assistants, and holds them in his person. It is for them he ascends the steps of the altar; it is their cause he is going to plead. He alone consecrates; but they all participate in the fruits of the offering. This is fully realized by the sacramental Communion—that precious practice which was general among the Christians of the first ages, and which has been preserved to a certain extent among Religious, even in our days of indifference and coldness. Three times a week, and sometimes oftener, the Professed thus unite themselves to the Priest in this great act; and when they are not allowed to receive sacramentally they do it spiritually—

that is to say, they endeavor to draw our Blessed Lord into their hearts by the fervor of their desires, feeding on the Sacrament in spirit by acts of lively faith and true charity, repeating in all humility the words of the centurion: *Domine, non sum dignus*—O Lord, I am not worthy; but say the word and my soul shall be cured. Each Communion day, for a true Religious, is a festival day, filling up his heart with unspeakable joys, and prompting him to an undying gratitude to God and a perfect fidelity to all his duties.

Day and night Jesus Christ resides in our tabernacles to give audience to those who visit Him, to receive and to grant their petitions, to enrich them with His most precious favors: "Come to Me, all you that labor, and are burdened, and I will refresh you." * Who could remain indifferent to such a loving invitation?

No Religious in the Congregation will ever let a single day pass without paying his homage to our Blessed Lord in the Sacrament of His love, for at least fifteen minutes. There can be no practice more consonant with reason, more useful, or more honorable and delightful. To visit Jesus Christ in the tabernacle has always been the sweetest joy of His true lovers. Some devout persons would remain almost constantly in the church, in order not to lose sight of the object of their love.

---

* St. Matth. xi, 28.

They make the church their cell and their chamber: a friend loves to dwell in the same room with the one he loves; a spouse can never be so happy as she is when with her bridegroom.

St. Francis Xavier, the Apostle of the Indies, lodged as near the church as he could, and slept in the sacristy. In the middle of the night he would go into the church and prostrate himself before the Blessed Sacrament. If, after praying for a long time, weariness and sleep overpowered him, he sank on the steps of the altar and took a little repose at the feet of his beloved Lord and Master.

RULE VIII.

Of Silence.

Every word that men shall speak, they shall render an account for it in the day of judgment.—*St. Matth.*, xii, 36.

Among the various causes that disgust sensible souls with a worldly life, the boisterous noise and incessant agitation, in which its votaries have to live, undoubtedly occupy a prominent place; and one of the principal charms with which a Religious life presents itself to their wearied imagination is the idea of peace, of solitude and silence, which will afford them rest, and facility to commune with themselves and with God, undisturbed and at leisure. A soul strongly impressed with the thought and conviction of the emptiness of the world, in which her nobler aspirations cannot be satisfied, feels the necessity of silence, that she may not be forced to live continually out of herself, but for herself and of her own life.

Such is the way by which most of us were induced to leave the world, and to seek God where we fancied we could find Him, "not in commotion," but in solitary and silent walks.

Such is indeed the inducement held out in a Community, and therefore such is the right of every Religious.

For the love of Jesus, who, to instruct us, and especially to show us the severity of His judgment against the abuses of the tongue, kept so long a silence at Nazareth, the members of the Community shall abstain from all unnecessary conversation at times and in places reserved for silence.

In regular Houses it is permitted to speak only during recreations. From night prayer until after Mass the next morning is the Great Silence. which can scarcely be violated without direct scandal.

The church or chapel in which the Blessed Sacrament is kept requires strict silence at all times. Then come in order, as places of silence, the vestry room, the Chapter room, the dormitories, refectories, corridors, private rooms, &c.

A Religious really a lover of silence will never disturb anyone unnecessarily, but will show his attention to it by the noiseless way he moves and acts, even in his walk, in opening or shutting a door; and in everything he does he will be eminently a man of silence—which means an interior man, living in God's holy presence—a man of faith, and whose every movement will be edifying to all around him.

Seldom has a man reason to fear for the silence he has kept; but many will find that an unbridled tongue is full of dangers, a source of remorse, and a prolific cause of sins.

Experience has long since clearly demonstrated that conversations not authorized by the Rule are not blessed, and not unfrequently sinful. Among the ordinary results of such indulgence are a loss of the spirit of recollection and union with God, the entering upon a spirit of dissipation, the lowering of respect for authority, the beginning of complaints and murmurs, an indifference for Religious regularity, and sometimes the ruin of vocations.

Silence favors serious and pious dispositions, but proves almost insupportable to frivolous, inconsistent and light heads.

RULE IX.

Of Humility.

Learn of Me, that I am humble of heart.—*St. Matth.* xi, 29.

Humility is the principle of all good, as pride is the origin of all sins. Hence it may be safely asserted that the Congregation will flourish or fail according as its members are humble or proud in the sight of God.

For their personal safety, they shall often meditate upon the humble and hidden life of Jesus Christ: on the astonishing annihilation of His Incarnation, of His Nativity, His Circumcision, His Presentation in the temple, His flight into Egypt, His sojourn at Nazareth, His Baptism, His temptation in the desert; on the manner He permitted men to judge Him and to treat Him through His public life, and especially during His Passion. In all temptations of vainglory and self-love they will have recourse to the Divine Master, saying from their hearts: "Jesus, humble of heart, have mercy on me."

In order to acquire humility they will accept with gratitude any little humiliations obedience may impose. Honors and dignities having been renounced by Profession, no one should ever attempt to take back with the left hand what he has offered with the right. No elevated post shall be sought or desired. No one will permit vainglory to follow and eat away the merit of his little successes, but all glory will be referred to God alone.

They will carefully avoid all manner of ostentation, and will ever cultivate modesty, as becomes Religious, in their countenance, in their dress, in their language, and, above all, in their heart.

RULE X.

Of the Spirit of Faith.

O Lord, do Thou increase my faith.—*St. Luke*, xvii, 5.

There is nothing so important, so absolutely necessary for the preservation and development of the Congregation, as the spirit of faith, especially in these days of indifference and apostasy, when those really possessed of that spirit are becoming so rare that we might well fear we had reached the time of which Jesus Christ once said: When the Son of man cometh, will He find, think you, faith on earth?* "Faith is the root and foundation of our justification," says the Council

* Luke, xviii, 8.

of Trent; hence without it we can do nothing for our own salvation or for the salvation of others; for without roots a tree can draw no sap from the earth, and without a foundation a building cannot be raised, or it falls. We must, therefore, frequently and fervently pray for an increase of faith, and then keep it alive by regular exercises and practices of piety, and especially by speaking of holy things in our conversations (which, alas! are so often turned on scandalous instead of edifying topics), and by spiritual readings. By these means faith may be kept alive, and bright, like a burning lamp which we always keep ready and well trimmed, to enlighten our steps in the path of righteousness.

He who possesses the spirit of faith is led in all things by the maxims and examples of the Saviour; the sense of God's presence animates his thoughts, his affections, his words, and all his acts and movements; "he lives by faith." Oh! the treasure—oh! the blessing such a Religious is in his Community! Let everyone often repeat the words of the Gospel: "I do believe, Lord; help Thou my unbelief."*

* Mark, ix, 23.

RULE XI.

Of Charity.

Thou shalt love the Lord Thy God with thy whole heart, and with thy whole soul,....and thy neighbor as thyself.—*St. Matth.*, xxii, 37, 39.

This Divine virtue consists in loving God, the Sovereign Good, for Himself, and ourself and our neighbor for God's sake. To fulfil this obligation as Jesus Christ has prescribed, each one shall endeavor as far as he can, with the aid of Divine grace, to perfect that love until it fills up his whole mind, his whole heart, and his whole strength. In regard to himself, a Religious would offend more or less should he neglect the care of his soul, or take an undue care of his body to the detriment of his soul. Therefore each one must follow obedience with regard to both his spiritual and bodily needs.

In reference to our neighbor, Jesus Christ has not ordained to love him as much as ourselves, but with a love similar though not equal to the love each has for himself, because we must always prefer our own eternal salvation to that of others. To accomplish the precept, no one should ever do to others what he would not like to have done to himself, and on the same principle should do to others precisely what he would wish to be done to himself.

Furthermore, as our Blessed Lord recommended to His disciples, the Congregation shall always try to render good for evil, whatever harm or injury may have been inflicted on its property or subjects.

"Charity," St. Paul says, "is patient, is kind: charity envieth not, dealeth not perversely, is not puffed up, is not ambitious, seeketh not her own, is not provoked to anger, thinketh no evil, rejoiceth not in iniquity, but rejoiceth with the truth: beareth all things, believeth all things, hopeth all things, endureth all things. Charity never falleth away."*

"Peace be to the brethren, and charity with faith," says the same Apostle, to the Ephesians.†

And again, to the Philippians: "This I pray, that your charity may more and more abound in knowledge, and in all understanding"‡; and in his second epistle to the Thessalonians he gives thanks to God because the charity of every one of them towards each other aboundeth. §

"Now," says he, (1 Tim. i, 5,) "the end of the commandment is charity from a pure heart."

What more can be needed to show the excellence of charity?

Above all, let the members of the Congregation have charity towards each other. Charity covers a multitude of sins and compensates for many deficiencies and imperfections before God and man.

---

* 1 Cor., xiii, 4-8. † vi, 23. ‡ i, 9. § i, 3.

RULE XII.

Of Meekness.

Learn of Me that I am meek.—*St. Matth.*, xi, 29.

Meekness is, in a manner, the flower of charity and the fruit of humility: it fills the soul with tender indulgence and pity, and spreads over the countenance an unfeigned pleasant grace, which is accompanied by a cordiality that inspires confidence and affection.

It enables a person to control an impetuous and angry temper, to bear injuries with patience, to disarm anger and insolence, to keep within the bounds of moderation and good breeding. It sets aside all airs of self-sufficiency and haughtiness, prevents sudden ebullitions of temper, harsh expressions, ill-mannered behavior, and those bursts of anger so humiliating afterwards to those who have been guilty of them, and so offensive even to their best friends.

"Blessed are the meek: for they shall possess the land"—or the hearts of the land. God will teach His ways to the meek; Moses was the meekest of all men. "It is better," says the Scripture, "to be humbled with the meek, than to divide spoils with the proud."*

---

* Proverbs, xvi, 19.

A Religious who has not yet learned how to govern his temper has something within himself sadly humiliating. Still, let him not despair of final success; St. Francis de Sales, a model of meekness, tells us that he was born with a violent temper, which for a long time gave him much trouble.

Let those who feel in danger of being carried away by any scandalous outburst of anger pray to God that they may appreciate meekness, and spare no efforts to obtain it. Let them foresee the occasions, and take timely and efficient measures to avoid them, or resist them victoriously when they do come. They will thus edify where they were wont to scandalize. They should make up their mind never to speak or to act whilst the storm of passion rages within, and they will find it profitable to raise their souls to God and say: O Jesus, meek and humble of heart, have pity on me! Another means to subdue an angry temper is to act honestly and offer an ample apology for the offence that may have been given.

RULE XIII.

Of the Spirit of Union and Community.

May they be one as We.—*St. John*, xvii, 11.

The spirit of the Congregation must be the

spirit of Jesus Christ, and all its members must be united together as were the disciples, for whom our Blessed Lord asked so earnestly of His heavenly Father this precious union, after having sent them to preach two by two, that they might keep unity of thoughts, of sentiments, and of actions.

It is union that gives power and success in worldly affairs; union likewise constitutes the happiness, the strength and glory of a Congregation, the minds and hearts of whose members are united in the soul of the Saviour as their bodies are united under the same roof and the same rule and discipline.

In order to preserve continually, and even to perfect, this inestimable union in the Congregation, all shall strive to imitate the harmonious understanding that exists among the various members of the body. According to St. Paul's declaration, they mutually help and serve each other: the eyes lead the feet; the hands protect the head; the strongest defend the weakest; the pain or enjoyment of one is common to the rest; and even in the distribution of food each member retains only what it needs, that all may receive an adequate share.

Moreover, to maintain in a Congregation the spirit of union and Community, it is necessary that the members should have and should testify great esteem for each other, and use among themselves the usual forms of politness and cordial affection which are found in families and circles of refined education, based on religious principles. Disputes, quarrels, ridiculing, all provocations to anger, must be forever banished from our mutual and daily intercourse.

Men of the world will sometimes resent an offence: in religion such a course can never be tolerated; when the offender has offered his apology, all is forgiven and must never be revived. A Religious whose heart is as it should be will not brood over an insult, real or imaginary; but he tries to derive from it all the merit which it presents. He complains of it to nobody, but thinks of it before the Blessed Sacrament, begging of our merciful Lord to forgive the offender as he forgives him, and to give him grace to do better.

Particular friendship with any one member is prohibited, because it is opposed to the spirit of community,—such a close union with one being a formal separation from the rest, in the same manner as organic and sensual affections weaken and even destroy union with God.

Any particular friendship dictated by ambition is no less to be blamed and condemned in a Community—where authority, if at all recognized as the expression of God's will, must be left entirely free.

An excessive love of parents or relatives is also an obstacle to the spirit of community; therefore it should not be forgotten that our Blessed Lord has declared those unworthy of Him who love father or mother, brothers or sisters, more than Him. This, however—by the grace of God—is here inserted rather as a warning than a reproach.

The better to imitate the life in common which Jesus Christ led with His apostles, a continual attention shall be paid to uniformity, which is the natural guardian of order and union. All singularity should be carefully avoided, in the food, in the dress and furniture, and even in the ordinary habits of life; because it more or less does away with the feeling that all the members form one family. Neither should there be singularity in exterior acts of mortification or devotion. The beauty of an army is the perfect uniformity of every soldier in dress, in arms, in movements, &c., &c. So likewise every Religious should be recognized at once, and everywhere, as a member of his Order,

---

RULE XIV.

Of Zeal.

I am come to cast fire on the earth; and what will I but that it be kindled?—*St. Luke*, xii, 49,

Zeal is that sacred fire spoken of by Jesus Christ; for it is like the flame of a devouring fire, and is in reality a holy excess of the love of God, and of souls, in a heart living by faith.

Indeed a Religious animated by the spirit of faith will never be able to think of the outrages offered to God by sin, and of the misfortune of the guilty, without feeling profoundly grieved, pouring forth fervent prayers, and afflicting himself by mortification. One thus possessed of the spirit of Jesus Christ will always be ready to devote himself, at any cost, to preach eternal truths, to form young hearts to virtue, to save souls and extend the Kingdom of God upon earth.

The same zeal will secure among teachers a discipline, order, regularity, devotedness to duty, and power of action to which all obstacles must yield. True zeal spares no pains. Whatever obedience is assigned to a zealous Religious, it will be a success. Such is the teaching of experience.

But zeal, to be efficient and according to God, must be regulated by wisdom and knowledge and that unction of charity which always seeks and finds a safeguard in obedience.

Care must be taken to avoid mistaking for zealous men those flighty and exalted heads whose ideas and schemes should rather be submitted to scrupulous examination than admitted to immediate execution.

In order to prevent the disorders and sad losses of an ill-directed zeal, no Religious shall undertake anything of his own accord; obedience, in

Religion, must regulate and sanction everything, whether in the Sacred Ministry, in teaching, or in any other employment.

RULE XV.

Of Mortification.

If any one will come after Me, let him deny himself, and take up his cross, and follow Me.—*St. Matthew*, xvi, 24.

Besides the Christian denial, which consists in abstaining from what is prohibited by God and by His Church, there is another, aiming at the practice of the evangelical counsels: in this we place religious mortification. By religious mortification the masters of spiritual life understand the habitual disposition, in a Religious, to deny himself unnecessary pleasure or bodily gratification, not authorized by the rules, to subdue his natural inclinations, his senses, his temper and humor, so as to be led no longer by the promptings of nature, but by faith. Such a mastery, however, must begin by a complete renouncing of all concupiscence of the flesh, of pride and all its suggestions, of ambition and its intrigues, and with a determination to gain it even by fast, discipline and haircloth, if necessary. No one shall practice any austerity without leave from his Director; but all are exhorted to bear, without complaint, heat and cold, sickness, fatigues, contradictions, humiliations, and whatever may cause pain to nature. Whoever wishes to advance in perfection will lead a mortified life, after the example of the Saints. Mortification is the mainspring of fervor.

In our time more than any other the aspirations of the age are to the reverse: the world is bent upon the enjoyments of the body.

The Religious of the Holy Cross—the followers, by choice and profession, of a crucified Master—will seek their delights where the Saints of all ages placed and found their delights.

RULE XVI.

Of Modesty.

Let your modesty be known to all men.—*Phil.*, iv, 5.

So great was the modesty impressed on the divine countenance of our Blessed Lord, that large crowds followed Him even to the desert, and thronged around Him, drawn and captivated by the charms not only of His eloquence but also of the extraordinary modesty of His whole person and demeanor.

The fruit of modesty is the fear of the Lord, riches and glory and life.*

In a Religious, modesty enhances every good quality, seals in him true merit, and gives him a mysterious charm which nothing else can impart.

A modest countenance is eminently apt to edify, to win confidence, and give a good name to a whole House or Community. It reveals at once a person considerate, humble, rather diffident, accustomed to interior and recollected habits, and naturally full of respect for others. Who would not prefer such a person to a boasting, bragging, proud, boisterous, imperious man, who seems to look down upon everybody as inferior to himself?

Any breach of modesty, either in words or dress or writings, or movements or acts, must be weighed according to its gravity. Before Profession, any serious doubt on this point commands a postponement of admission. It is considered contrary to religious modesty to speak too loud, to interrupt another in conversation, to run without necessity, to touch another by way of joke or play, to go out before being fully dressed, to lounge on two chairs, to cross one leg over the other, to talk noisily in company, to whistle, &c. &c., to spit on the floor in church, parlor, regular places, corridors, stairs, &c.

A sense of propriety will supply the rest.

---

* Prov., xxii, 4.

RULE XVII.

Of Regular Discipline.

One jot or one tittle shall not pass from the law, till all be fulfilled.—*Matth.*, v, 18.

Regularity in a Congregation is the prompt obedience of all to the Rules. It would seem that after Profession, by which a Religious has bound himself to obedience, there should be no further need to impress on him the importance of regularity. Regularity is the most prolific source of consolations to a Religious heart; by it he constantly feeds his soul and edifies the Community.

To be regular, one must follow daily, from the first moment to the last, from 5 until 9, all the exercises of the House where he lives. Whoever comes in after the beginning of an exercise, the president excepted, kisses the floor. Every absence requires a previous permission or an immediate excuse.

The regularity of a Religious should not be that of a slave; it should spring from more elevated motives. It should be dictated by faith, which ennobles everything it prompts.

One of the best means to maintain discipline in a Community is the Chapter of Accusations every Friday; next come the Monthly Retreat, Monition, and Direction.

There is a sense of pleasure, which is as natural

as it is commendable, in the fact of belonging to a House of which everyone speaks well; and, on the other hand, it is no small humiliation to one of feeling to know that his House has a bad name everywhere as a relaxed House. Let it be borne in mind that the one and the other attach to discipline chiefly. Without discipline a House has no chance whatever. Here is the primary element of success; without it nothing can be expected but dishonor, disaster, and ruin.

RULE XVIII.

Of the Studies in the Congregation.

My doctrine is not Mine, but of Him that sent Me.
—*St. John*, vii, 16.

So admirable was the doctrine of Jesus Christ that the Jews who listened to Him could not help exclaiming: How can this man know the Scriptures, who has not studied them? It was true, He had never studied them; but He proclaimed as man what He knew as God.

Since original sin has disturbed everything, study has become a necessity for man in order to acquire knowledge. Unless destined for manual labor, the Religious of the Holy Cross shall apply themselves in earnest to the studies which obedience shall have marked out, strictly following the plan and method adopted by the Congregation.

It is much to be desired that even the Brothers not destined to teach should know or learn reading, writing, and ciphering. They should all be well instructed in religion and in the duties of a religious life.

The Brothers preparing to teach shall be fully trained up after a determined system, in order to cope with the teachers in public schools.

The Ecclesiastics, after finishing their classical course, shall study Philosophy at least one year; and for three years they shall follow a regular course of Dogmatic and Moral Theology, Holy Scriptures, Ceremonies, Rubrics, and Plain Chant. In none of these branches should anything be spared to impart a thorough education, unless pride or lack of ability forbid.

The sphere of knowledge in our plan of studies being large, and the system or method practical and clear, nothing is wanting to secure the contemplated object but to follow it in earnest, instead of studying at random one thing to-day and another to-morrow, without rule or direction, and with neither result nor merit. There must be *system* in studies, more than in anything else; otherwise time is lost and no satisfaction obtained. Nor should it ever be imagined that in order to complete an education a Religious may freely use all sorts of books. A pure heart will always find it unnecessary to handle a polluting work of any sort.

No publication should ever be undertaken by any member of the Congregation without the ordinary *permissu superiorum* required in all Religious Orders.

Above all, let every study in the Congregation be based on the spirit of prayer, which is a fountain of light: let it begin, and continue, and end in the same holy disposition. God will bless those whose studies shall be thus permeated by such continual pious aspirations; and while their minds will be enriched with precious knowledge their hearts will not, as it frequently happens, suffer an irreparable shipwreck of piety.

RULE XIX.

Of Recreations and Conversations.

And He conversed with men.—*Baruch*, iii, 38.

Recreation is to recreate: it is no waste of time; it is a means to keep in a healthy condition both mind and body, neither of which can be constantly and heavily taxed without injury.

Jesus Christ, our Model in all circumstances of life, has taught us by His example how to converse and how to keep silence. Him therefore we should try to imitate in our conversations and recreations. For His sake, and in imitation of Him, all should be attentive to cultivate in recreation modesty, charity, justice, truth, patience and forbearance, and to show themselves as sociable and entertaining as possible to their companions.

Recreations are spent in common; and in this the Rule requires something more than the bodily presence of all members; some efforts must be made to create an interest in those regular and social meetings, which otherwise would soon prove dull and monotonous. It is scarcely admissible that one should be there as a log, for half an hour or more, without giving the company any sign of interest or pleasure; of such a Religious nobody could say that he is very amiable.

Conversational powers are no common gift, especially among men meeting daily in the same circle. Once more let everyone bear in mind that each Religious must bring his quota to render Recreations lively and exhilarating to all.

There are also things to be avoided in Recreation—namely: untruthfulness, haughtiness, sarcasm, censuirng, complaining of the administration, &c., &c., speaking in a loud or angry tone, disputing or contesting in offensive words, relating scandals, or insinuating suspicions unworthy of a

Christian heart, &c., &c. Unless a scrupulous watchfulness be used, one may lose in a quarter of an hour's recreation the fruit of many months' efforts and resolutions. Let everyone go to Recreation in obedience to the Rule, with a view to improve the social feelings of the Community, to recreate and make mirthful and happy everyone around him, to edify all, and make them feel indeed how good and how pleasant it is for brethren to dwell together in unity.* A talented Religious, truly possessed of the spirit of his Order, is nowhere more useful to his Community than in Recreation. Fénélon, the saintly Archbishop of Cambray, who probably never was surpassed in conversational powers, and who never grieved anyone, but made all feel better and more delighted, drew from his own loving heart inexhaustible means of winning to God everyone who came in contact with him. A few men thus disposed, and possessed of zeal and ability, might within a few months, and in Recreation alone, change and amend the tone and sentiments of a whole Community.

Ecclesiastical history, the Lives of the Saints, the edifying movements and actions of nations and individuals towards God and His Vicar on earth, are prolific topics from which a well-read person will draw, with little effort, and day after

---

* Psalm cxxxii, 1.

day, something new, instructive, and full of interest for all around him.

A man of honor will never permit in his presence any conversation tending to lessen due respect for authority, charity to equals, or justice to anybody.

With the right man present, Recreations are spent both innocently and interestingly.

RULE XX.

Of Fraternal Correction.

If thy brother shall offend against thee, go and rebuke him, between thee and him alone. If he shall hear thee, thou shalt gain thy brother. But if he will not hear thee, take with thee one or two more, . . . and if he will not hear them, tell the church.

—*St. Matth.*, xviii, 15–17.

Thus our Blessed Lord declared the duty and the mode of fraternal correction. Accordingly, every Religious must be ready to receive advice and admonition, and even give it, as the case may be. But in order that this important and delicate obligation be fulfilled in prudence and charity, the following rule should be strictly adhered to:

If anyone be guilty of a slight transgression, the first opportunity shall be availed of to call his attention thereto, kindly and mildly. If the fault is serious, but secret, he who shall have noticed it will speak to the offender privately and alone. If no amendment is obtained, then he shall inform the Monitor of the party; and if this prove useless, the Superior must be made aware of what has passed. Then the Superior takes it in his own hands. But if the transgression has been public, and somewhat scandalous, the same process is followed up, with an earnestness proportionate to the gravity of the case; and if no improvement is perceived, then a public monition must be given in Chapter, after the apostolic counsel: "Them that sin reprove before all, that the rest also may have fear." *

Very grave charges must be very seriously examined and weighed ere they are credited. But when anyone has been convicted of the transgression of the Rule, prompt action alone will prove that authority is not indifferent to good or evil. In such cases, postponement is the ruin of religious discipline. Allowance must be made for age, dispositions, ignorance, temptation, provocation, circumstances, actual sorrow, &c., for there is a wide difference between one who repents and another remaining obstinate. A first pardon is even advisable; but to pardon a fault honestly acknowledged, and to let it pass unnoticed, are two

* 1 Timothy, v, 20.

things very different: the former, while saving the subject, invigorates discipline; the latter kills both the one and the other.

There is a special Monitor named at the General Retreat for the Fathers, and another for the Brothers, in every separate House. Every Religious, Superiors not excepted, must have his Monitor, and see him monthly. Monitors are the mainstay of Religious Discipline in a Congregation, provided they discharge their office with zeal and charity, politeness and humility.

Tale-bearers are detestable, everywhere; but informing Superiors of what they should know, for the good of a House, is no tale-bearing. If a first information appear to have been overlooked, let it be reiterated; if again disregarded, let it be carried to a superior officer, as the Provincial or Superior General.

Whoever receives an admonition should sincerely and heartily thank him who imparts it. It is no time to contest, but to listen to and profit by what is stated. Between two Religious, a monition never creates anything but good feelings. It should last but a few minutes, and, if more convenient, can be transmitted in writing, in two or three lines.

This Rule on Monition should not be construed as stepping on the following, from which it essentially differs.

RULE XXI.

Of the Direction.

If the blind lead the blind, both fall into the pit.
—*St. Matthew*, xv, 14.

God having established that man should be saved by man, and the Holy Ghost exhorting us to seek the counsel of the wise and that of the ancients, it is not to be wondered at if our Blessed Lord insists in the Gospel that the blind should not be led by the blind. Hence the advice of St. Francis de Sales to choose a Director from among a thousand.

In the Novitiates, Postulants and Novices shall apply for Direction to the Master of Novices, and in other Houses to the Superior of each House, every month. Direction consists in revealing to a Director, confidentially, but candidly, how the one asking Direction feels, and how much satisfied with himself in the manner he serves God; if he be at peace with himself and with everybody; if he attends regularly all the exercises of the Community, or loses any by his own fault; if he finds it difficult to lead a life of obedience, and in what he fails chiefly; if he meets in his employment with any particular danger or difficulty; or if he is as fervent and desirous of advancing in perfection as ever, or less, and why; if the interests of the Congregation are as dear to his heart as before.

Many a soul, says St. Francis de Sales, has obtained salvation through the means of Direction. Whoever in a Community would pass it by, whatever the motive may be (and in nine cases out of ten it is pride or indifference), is neither right nor safe. Direction, however, is not Confession.

RULE XXII.

Of Confession.

Thy sins are forgiven thee.—*St. Matthew*, ix, 2.

The happiness experienced by the poor man sick of the palsy on hearing the Saviour assuring him of the forgiveness of his sins, may be shared in by anyone who has recourse to the ministry of the priests; for He has delegated to them the same power He Himself used towards the unfortunate man sick of the palsy.

All go to Confession every week, to the Confessor appointed. Much depends on the preparation, by which abundant fruits may be secured and the danger of routine avoided.

An extraordinary Confessor shall be named, to afford every Religious an opportunity for an extraordinary Confession in the Ember Weeks.

True Religious are generally easily satisfied with the Confessor given them.

For the rest, all are referred to the *Directory*.

RULE XXIII.

Of the Chapter of Accusations.

He that humbleth himself shall be exalted.
—*St. Luke*, xviii, 14.

This declaration of Jesus Christ finds its verification especially in the spontaneous, humble, and honest accusation by Religious of the faults they have committed against the Rules, and by which they have more or less disedified if not scandalized the members of the Community where they live. By thus acknowledging, of their own accord, their weekly failings, they often greatly edify while they give a salutary warning to others, they frequently strengthen discipline, and gain even more than they had lost in the esteem of others; above all, they recover thereby the peace of conscience which had been disturbed, and they are relieved from the responsibiltiy which attaches to every public transgression until such an apology shall have been offered.

Every Religious shall make his accusation weekly, and receive in a spirit of humility the penance the president will impose, which penance must be proportionate to the gravity of the faults.

Accusations in Chapter are divided into three classes: namely,—slight faults, grave faults, and very serious faults; to which are three kinds of corresponding penances.

1st.—Slight transgressions: To speak in time of silence, or in places where it is forbidden; to come too late to an exercise; to show some levity in the church, or during a regular exercise; to walk too fast; to open and shut the doors without attention; to take too little, or too much, care of personal dress; to speak too much, and inconsiderately; to be wanting in exterior modesty; to take but little care of the obedience assigned; to show some indifference to the Rules, or to the interests of the Congregation; &c.

For such faults the following penances shall be imposed: namely,—to say the Litany of Loretto; to make a visit to the Blessed Sacrament; to recite a decade of the Beads.

2d.—The grave transgressions are: To rise habitually too late; to be absent from Meditation or other Community exercises without leave or excuse; to pay little attention to the recommendations of Superiors; to disregard the Great Silence; to enter the room of a companion in his absence and search through his papers and things; to keep a lighted candle or lamp after having gone to bed;

to sow seeds of division in a Community; to offend in words or writings against truth, charity, modesty, &.; to censure the acts of Councils and Superiors; to cause, by neglect, damage or loss to the Community. Against these faults the following penances shall be imposed: namely,—to say the Beads two or three times; to recite the Seven Penitential Psalms; to make one hour of adoration; &c.

3.—Should a Religious forget himself so far as to continue in any of the grave faults above mentioned; or disobey the orders of a Superior; or work against lawful authority, or against the peace or order of a House, directly or indirectly; or intercept letters of Superiors, or to Superiors; or grievously insult anyone, or try to destroy anyone's character; visit or correspond with, after being prohibited, persons considered dangerous; or remain absent longer than permitted; or appropriate money without leave; refuse the statistics of a House or the accounts of an administration of which he has charge; or make expenses not authorized; or contract debts without due permission; change the Rules for the diet or vestiary; exhibit habitually no regularity, especially in the rising, and in the retiring to bed; keep liquors secreted, or give way to intemperance; or give scandal in any notorious way,—which God forbid!—the prayers of the Community should be asked for his amendment, and he should be separated, if in any way possible, from the rest of his companions, until a sensible change shall have taken place in his unfortunate dispositions. He should be placed upon a Retreat, for a week or two; and in case he should remain obstinate and unchanged, the insignia of his Profession should be taken away from him, and the case referred to the Provincial.

The accusations in Chapter being as it were a public confession, whoever should, at any time, reveal anything said or done there, would simply dishonor himself.

RULE XXIV.

Of the Monthly Retreat.

Come apart into a desert place, and rest a little.
St. Mark, vi, 31.

On the first Sunday of each month all attend in silence the Monthly Retreat, a practice the importance of which can hardly be overrated either by Superiors or by simple Religious. On this day they hear Jesus Christ Himself inviting by name every Religious of the Congregation to "come apart and rest a little" with Him. This Retreat will be for each one a pause or a halt, to cast back a glance upon the distance just run over, and survey the space that lies immediately before them. The *Directory* fully explains how to proceed on the occasion.

Were it not for the Monthly Retreat but few in a Community could preserve the spirit of fervor imparted by the Annual Retreat.

The life of Religious in the Congregation is, generally speaking, so completely filled with duties—and exposed, at the same time, to the wear and tear of such exterior and incessant contact with the world—that unless the soul be called back into solitude once in a while, every interior disposition gradually gives way.

Hence the necessity of the Monthly Retreat must be obvious to all who honestly desire to see the Congregation safe against the dangers above mentioned, and likewise against what is no less to be dreaded, the natural bent of poor human nature, everywhere inclined to evil, and its inherent inconstancy and manifold slight infidelities, which daily weaken divine grace even in fervent souls.

RULE XXV.

Of the Feasts of the Congregation.

Go you to this festival day.—*St. John*, vii, 8.

By thus commanding His disciples to go to the

feast of the tabernacles, Jesus Christ intended to impress upon all minds the importance of religious solemnities, which in the New Law excel anything that existed in the Old Dispensation, as much as the reality excels the figure. Indeed among the various means by which the Church keeps up and increases the fervor of her children, one of the most efficient is the solemnity with which she celebrates the memory of her chief Mysteries and of her most glorious Saints.

Hence the devotion with which we should commemorate the great Festivals of the Church; and also those peculiar to the Congregation,—namely, that of the Sacred Heart of Jesus, the titular Feast of the Congregation and the Patronal one of the Priests; that of St. Joseph, the Patronal of the Brothers; the Festival of Our Lady of the Seven Dolors, by which the Congregation is associated with the Blessed Virgin in honoring with her, and under her guidance and protection, the great mystery of the Holy Cross to which it is dedicated.

The above are the three principal solemnities of the Congregation. They are preceded by a fast, that greater blessings may be derived from them.

The Month of the Holy Infancy, the Month of St. Joseph, and the Month of Mary, are now practices of piety too general among Catholics to be any longer considered devotions special to the Congregation. The more, however, they gain ground, the more fervently and thankfully they should be kept in all the Houses of the Holy Cross.

RULE XXV.

Of the Vows.

Come, and follow Me.—*St. Matthew*, xix, 21.

The young man to whom Jesus Christ addressed the above words had been from his infancy a faithful observer of all the Commandments; but he yet knew not the evangelical counsels, by which he was invited to follow the Saviour more perfectly, by imitating His poverty, His chastity, and His obedience. These are the most excellent virtues, called of counsel because not of command; their profession constitutes the essence of Religious life.

Therefore whoever has understood this sublime doctrine, and feels sufficient courage to accept it, must lead a life of poverty, chastity, and obedience, according to the Rules of the Society into which he has been received.

Such is the life the Religious of the Holy Cross have chosen: they enter upon it immediately after their Novitiate by yearly vows at first, and then by their Profession.

The annals of Communities mention cases of

Religious making their Profession without any intention of binding themselves. The Gospel, too, relates the treason of Judas.

The virtue and the obligation of a vow are different from each other: for instance, the vow of obedience *obliges* only the material fulfilment of orders, while the virtue of the same vow inclines the will to obey promptly, gladly, zealously, perfectly.

RULE XXVI.

Of the Vow of Poverty.

The Son of man hath not whereupon to rest His head.—*St. Matthew* viii, 20.

Whereas civil laws do not recognize everywhere, at this present time, all the effects of this important vow, a Novice in the Congregation of the Holy Cross might, strictly speaking, make his Profession and yet retain in his name the deed or deeds of his property; but in this case it must be clearly understood that by the vow of poverty he renounces the liberty to administer or use it except in entire dependence of the Superior General. It is a right of which certain civil laws sometimes prevent the complete sacrifice; but one of which no use whatever can be made by a Religious except with the full consent of Superiors.

For a true Religious, who enters the Congregation with proper dispositions, the above reserve will never amount to anything: the sacrifice was complete in his heart; and although some property may remain vested in his name, the administration of it is freely left to the Community. Should he come into possession of, or inherit any property, even after his Profession, having once given up all riches to follow Jesus Christ he leaves it all to his Superiors, or to those entitled by his testament to share in it. He remains, in practice, as poor as though he had never owned a farthing.

No Religious should receive a present of any sort on condition of reserving it to his own exclusive use: it would be a direct violation of his vow. Whatever is offered to a Religious, if accepted with proper leave, is received for God and the Congregation. Superiors determine the use of it as they may see fit.

Whatever profit may arise from private industry, composition or publication of books, &c., belongs by right to the Community.

The Rules determine what is necessary concerning the food, the clothing and furniture, and all should be not only satisfied with it, but unwilling to create a precedent on a point of such delicacy by objecting to the regulations already made.

Money received for a journey, or for any special

object, cannot be employed otherwise without a violation of the vow.

The vow of poverty furthermore obliges one not to retain for personal use anything costly, even among objects of piety; to make or receive no present; to dispose of nothing, directly or otherwise; and never to indulge unnecessary expenses, whether at home or on a journey.

The spirit of the Congregation regarding real estate and other property is that no Superiors should hold any in their individual names; but civil and legal corporations must be formed, were it only to hold possession of what goods may accrue to the Congregation.

Such corporations are composed exclusively of the members of the Community, and their statutes must be sanctioned by the Superior General.

The conscience of Superiors and Directors is charged, from the day of their election, with a fearful responsibility. Indeed if during their administration the spirit of poverty should—which God forbid—die away among the members, the destiny of the Congregation should be in the greatest danger; and unless a Superior be continually watching, and determined to struggle against the strong current of the age—unless he is prepared "to reprove in time and out of time" in order to preserve and keep intact this indispensable foundation of Religious life—soon, very soon indeed, the love of ease and comfort, the fear of pain and fatigue, will take the place of devotedness, the idea of sacrifice will gradually disappear, and all will be lost.

The budget, once duly sanctioned, should not be exceeded in any Establishment.

In every House the details of the administration are regulated by the strictest economy; and whatever surplus remains at the close of each year belongs by right to the Provincial Council, with which the General Administration deals.

The better to secure the observance of the vow of poverty, so replete with serious consequences in a Community, all should endeavor to practise the virtue of poverty, by suppressing every undue attachment to anything and by preferring for personal use whatever is inferior in quality. Upon a constant fidelity to this practice depend the peace of conscience, the edification of all and the blessing of God on the Congregation. Who will comprehend and scrupulously observe this? Ah! surely not the worldly-minded, the lukewarm, nor the nominal or half Religious,—but the man of faith, who places the soul above the body—the superior mind, whose clear and far-seeing eye foresees the success or the ruin of his Congregation attached to the observance or disregard of the vow of poverty. Fortunately, the presence of one true lover of poverty among many is sometimes sufficient to preserve the spirit of the vow.

RULE XXVII.

Of the Vow of Chastity.

They are as the angels in heaven.—*St. Mark*, xii, 25.

If by the Sixth and Ninth Commandments God forbids all men the pleasures of the flesh; if this kind of sin admits of no levity of matter even in a common Christian, how much purer should be the hearts of those who, adding the vow to the precept, profess to imitate the angels in their conduct, and to follow the spotless Lamb whom virgins alone can approach.

Such is, indeed, the object of the vow of chastity, by which one engages himself to live free from wilful stain, raised above the carnal desires and concupiscences of the earth, not alone in imagination or in the affections of the heart, but also in words, in looks, in actions, in gestures, and in all that makes up the man exteriorly and interiorly.

To remain true to such sacred engagements, each Religious will carefully observe sobriety and temperance; will be modest before all, and make free with none; will not touch anyone, even by way of play; will not receive children in his room with doors closed; will not kiss them except on rare occasions, viz., meeting them after an absence or bidding them adieu. Particular friendship with any of them is strictly forbidden.

Novels, light reading, paintings, engravings, or statues, in any way objectionable to a pure soul, shall not be retained.

Persons of another sex shall neither be visited alone nor corresponded with unnecessarily and without a special permission. Religious receive no visits in their own rooms, but in common parlors. Wherever our Religious give or receive services to or from Sisters, the Superiors will see that the greatest prudence be observed to protect the virtue and reputation of all.

RULE XXVIII.

Of the Vow of Obedience.

I seek not My own will.—*St. John*, v, 30.

Such was the self-denial of our Blessed Lord that He could truly say, speaking of His Father: "I do His will always." It is precisely what a good Religious can also say, who, wishing to remain faithful to his vows, obeys his Superiors promptly, constantly, supernaturally, and devotedly.

By the vow of obedience a Religious consecrates to God his entire will, and renounces the right of following the promptings of his desires and personal inclinations except in complete subservience to lawful authority.

By their Profession the Religious of the Holy Cross pledge a filial obedience to the Holy See, to the General Chapter, to the Superior General regularly elected and confirmed by the Holy Father, and likewise to all Superiors lawfully named and commanding within the limits of their office. They submit themselves also not only to the Constitutions and Rules now in force, but also to Statutes and Decrees which in course of time may be enacted by General Chapters.

Although there are no Rules obligatory of themselves under pain of sin except those treating of the vows, it would be sinful, however, to violate any Rule through pride or contempt of authority, through sensuality, sloth, human respect, or any other vicious motive. It would be the same if, in disregarding a Rule, one would expose himself to the danger of falling into a grievous sin, or giving scandal, or of causing some damage to the Congregation or to a neighbor.

All should yield such a ready obedience as to render any command unnecessary. As soon as the Superior's will is known, it should be executed with an unfeigned submission of both the will and the understanding.

In order to be confirmed in the virtue of obedience, everyone shall be guarded against criticism, prejudice or murmuring; also against all servile fear, or a personal love of ease.

If refused by one Superior, a subject should not

apply to another without informing him of the previous refusal.

Superiors will endeavor to blend firmness and meekness, the former being indispensable to the maintenance of discipline, and the latter largely contributing to render obedience easy and authority paternal and loved. They must not overlook a point of serious gravity—viz., that they will never obtain universal obedience more readily from those placed under their jurisdiction than when they themselves show their respect for the same Rules and their entire submission to higher Superiors.

No Superior shall be considered as commanding under pain of mortal sin unless when he says: "I command in virtue of Holy Obedience," or "in the name of Jesus Christ."

RULE XXIX.

Of Admission to Vows.—Of the Profession and Ordinations.

Unless the grain of wheat falling into the ground, die, itself remaineth alone.—*St. John*, xii, 24, 25.

In order to die to the world and to themselves, with Jesus Christ, and to secure an abundance of eternal fruits, the Josephite Brothers who have completed their Novitiate make for one year the vows of Poverty, Chastity and Obedience, in the hands of their Superior. The Salvatorists under age likewise make the yearly vows.

The fulfilment of all conditions for the Profession is certified to the Superior General in due time, by the Provincial, in his Council: in this official communication on the Novice he shall state his age; that he has been under the three vows for twelve months (if a Josephite); that he passed a regular examination two months before the end of his Novitiate, before the Provincial Council, whom he satisfied as to his science, his conduct and religious dispositions; that he is possessed of testimonial letters, and not bound by any impediment; and, finally, that he has satisfactorily regulated his temporal affairs.

The Salvatorists may make their Profession at the close of their Novitiate, if of age.

The final admission is decided by the Superior General in his Council, by a vote of two thirds, and is immediately notified to the Provincial.

As soon as the Profession shall have been made, the Provincial shall communicate the same to the Superior General.

When vows are pronounced by Novices, the formula must be written or at least signed by them, and preserved in the archives of the Province.

The emission of perpetual vows is preceded by a retreat of six days, during which, if they have not done so before, the Novices shall dispose, by testament or otherwise, of their temporal goods, according to the spirit of the Rules and with the full agreement of the Provincial or Superior.

Yearly, at the close of the General Retreat, all renew their vows in the hands of the Provincial or local Superior.

No Ecclesiastical Novice can be offered for ordination without a previous examination, as shall be presently explained, and without a proper retreat.

Every candidate for ordination must bring to the Ordinary by whom he is to be ordained a dimissory letter from the Superior General. No one can be ordained without it. The following treatises shall be presented for examination in this Order: viz., *Catechism* and *Christian Doctrine*, fully explained, for Tonsure; *de Religione et Ecclesiâ*, for Minor Orders; *de Deo, de Trinitate, de Fide, de Incarnatione, de Gratiâ et de Sacramentis in genere*, for Subdeaconship; *de Actibus Humanis, de Conscientiâ, de Legibus, de Peccatis et Decalogo*, for Deaconship; *de Baptismo, de Confirmatione, de Extrema Unctione, de Pœnitentiâ, de Indulgentiis, de Ordine, de Matrimonio, de Jure, de Contractibus, de Censuris et Irregularitatibus*, and finally *de Ceremoniis et Liturgiâ.*

RULE XXX.

Of the Dismissal of Subjects.

If he hears not the Church, let him be to thee as a heathen and a publican.—*St. Matthew*, xviii, 17.

A postulant is dismissed by the Provincial upon the testimony of the Master who had him in charge; a Novice, by the Provincial in his Council, upon the report of the Master of Novices; a Novice out of the novitiate and under vows, by the Provincial in his Council, after obtaining of the Superior General a proper dispensation from vows. Upon the reception of this dispensation, the Local Council of the House in which said Novice lives meets again to examine the case anew: if two thirds of the votes are against him, the same is immediately communicated to the Provincial, who finally pronounces his dismissal and orders its execution.

As to Professed, if such an unfortunate member should ever be found so entirely lost to all sense of religion as to require expulsion, Constitution XXII should be scrupulously followed and and carried out. Prudence, charity, and a desire to avoid scandal, will show the Administration what course to follow in the removal of one so greatly to be pitied.

No communication whatever can be kept with any Religious regularly dismissed.

RULE XXXI.

Of the Order of the Day.

Let every thing be done in order.—1 *Cor.*, xiv, 40.

St. Paul, in prescribing to the Corinthians to do everything orderly and decently, has traced out the way which all the Religious of the Holy Cross should follow.

To secure to all the same advantages of a regular and Religious life, they shall be governed, wherever they are, by the same regulations, viz.: 5 o'clock, Rising; 5.30, Meditation; 6, Holy Mass; 7, Breakfast; 11.45, Particular Examen; 12, Dinner, followed by one hour Recreation; 6.30, Supper, followed by Recreation; Spiritual Reading, Evening Prayer, and Points for next Meditation, at 8; last bell, ten minutes after Night Prayer.

From Easter until the General Retreat the rising is at 4.30.

At dinner and supper a portion of the *New Testament* (from ten to twelve verses) is read first; then the life of some Saint. At the end of dinner the *Martyrology* is read, and at supper ten or twelve lines of the *Rules*. In small Establishments the reading of the Life of a Saint is omitted.

The Beads are said in common a quarter of an hour before the Spiritual Reading.

All should try to meet together in the Chapel, for the Visit, at a quarter before supper.

The Fathers should always have the Little Hours said before breakfast, and the rest of the Divine Office at the earliest possible hour. The same applies to teaching Brothers, for the Little Office.

Unless prevented by personal duty, or the requirements of society with strangers, silence shall be kept except in Recreation hours.

In each House one member is appointed by the Superior to see that all rise and retire according to Rule.

RULE XXXII.

Of the Rank in the Congregation.

When thou art invited to a wedding, sit not down in the first place, lest perhaps one more honorable than thou be invited by him; and he that invited thee and him, come and say to thee, Give this man place: and then thou begin with shame to take the lowest place.
—*St. Luke*, xiv, 8, 9.

To avoid the shame spoken of in the above text by our Blessed Lord, and preserve order in the assemblies of the Congregation, each one shall take his place as follows: viz.: The Salvatorists at the right hand of the president, and the Josephites at the left, each and all in the order indicated in Constitution XXIII. In the case of two or more members of different Houses having been professed on the same day, they rank according to the priority of foundation of the Houses to which they belong.

There is in each Province and in each House a list of members, renewed yearly, by which everyone's place is fixed.

RULE XXXIII.

Of Meals, and Food in General.

Be not solicitous therefore, saying, what shall we eat: or what shall we drink, or wherewith shall we be clothed?—*St. Matth.*, vi, 31.

While praising the austerities of the Precursor, who neither eat bread nor drank wine, and though practising prayer and mortification when alone, Jesus Christ presents Himself as a model of the common life of a Religious, as He lived with His Apostles, and conformed to the usages of the country.

In imitation of the Divine Model, each one shall always show himself satisfied with what may be placed on the table. In case of sickness, the doctor's prescriptions shall be strictly observed in candor and simplicity.

Three meals a day, taken in common and at regular hours, form the *régime* of the Community. Religious of a feeble constitution may be allowed, especially in summer, to take a lunch at 4 P. M. The same may be taken by those whose duties or labors are very severe.

Breakfast consists of a dish of meat, with bread and butter and coffee.

Dinner: of soup, a dish of roast meat or a *ragout*, two dishes of vegetables, and dessert.

At supper: a dish of meat, with butter or cheese or some vegetables, and tea.

Except in Colleges, strangers shall not be invited to meals in our Houses.

Travelling Religious should always be received with courteous hospitality.

A wholesome diet, sufficient and palatable without extra expense, and economy blended with taste, will always reveal in a Superior an administrator of no ordinary feeling and ability, who cares for his Religious and yet wastes none of the funds of the Community.

RULE XXXIV.

Of the Vestiary.

Be not solicitous for your life, what you shall eat, nor for your body, what you shall put on. Is not the life more than the meat; and the body more than the raiment?—*St. Matth.*, vi, 25.

The Religious of the Holy Cross being all alike the children of one family, their clothes and linen are kept in a common clothes-room. These are made of the same material, according to a fixed rule or style, as prescribed by the Provincial Chapter in each Province, and distributed weekly in the same quantity to all.

Every Religious has a Number, with which all his effects are marked. Care is taken that the vestiary be preserved with perfect cleanliness.

Each Religious is provided with precisely what the Rule prescribes, neither more nor less. When a Religious is moved to another House, he takes with him his own wardrobe.

The wardrobe of a Religious of the Holy Cross is composed of the following articles,—viz.:

For the Fathers—2 cassocks and 2 capes, one for summer and another for winter; 2 pairs of pantaloons, 4 pairs of drawers, 1 cord, 1 crucifix, 2 pairs of shoes, 1 hat and 1 cap, 6 shirts, 4 woollen shirts, 6 pairs of stockings, 6 pocket-handkerchiefs, 1 overcoat, 12 collars, 1 biretta,—each of the above articles to be made in the same style and of the same material for all. Simplicity, solidity and modesty take here the place of costly and fashionable clothes worn by persons of the world, who would feel scandalized at a Religious dressed like a worldly man.

For the Brothers—2 habits, one for summer and another for winter; 2 pairs of pantaloons, 4 pairs of drawers, 1 cord, 1 statuette of St. Joseph, 2 pairs of shoes, 1 hat, 1 cap, 6 shirts, 4 woollen shirts, 6 pairs of stockings, 6 pocket-handkerchiefs, 1 overcoat, 12 collars, 1 religious cap,—each of the above articles to be made alike and of the same material and with the same restrictions as above.

While Religious should carefully guard against all worldly airs in dress and manners, they must equally avoid appearing repulsive, or in any way dirty, slovenly, or even negligent in dress.

Superiors cannot be too vigilant in maintaining uniformity in the vestiary of their Religious; for there are everywhere eccentric minds who, if left free, would not leave a vestige of uniformity in a Community in the course of a few years. A Congregation respecting itself will allow no such deviation from its Rules, and the best members will never bear to see their Religious costume trifled with and dishonored by flighty and ridiculous dandies who still wish to be called Religious.

In every Provincial House there are samples and models stamped, and to which all conform.

RULE XXXV.

Of Furniture.

Let us therefore make him a little chamber, and put a little bed in it for him, and a table, and a stool, and a candlestick, that when he cometh to us he may abide there.—4 *Kings*, iv, 10.

What sufficed to the prophet Eliseus, who was a figure of Jesus Christ, should certainly suffice to Religious, who have made a special vow to practise poverty.

Through respect for the Priests' sacred character, a private room is given to every Father of the Congregation. Besides the bed, the table, and three chairs, there must be in each room a praying-desk, a clothes-press, a toilet table and a mirror, a few book-shelves, a crucifix, and one or two pictures of piety. Nothing costly—and yet decent, and kept perfectly neat.

The Brothers sleep in common dormitories, well ventilated and comfortable, and study in a common study-room, in which each has a desk, books, paper and ink, and everything necessary to employ usefully his spare hours, while the working members rest or read in a common exercise-room, where they may, when their task is over, spend some moments every day in reading or praying, without hindrance or annoyance of any sort.

The above rooms must be kept scrupulously clean and well aired. The walls are adorned with some large religious engravings, and a crucifix or a little oratory towards which all turn for prayer and to which they bow when they go in and out. In all Community rooms silence, neatness, purity of air, comfort and edification must be found.

RULE XXXVI.

Intercourse with Persons Outside.

So let your light shine before men, that they may see your good works, and glorify your Father who is in heaven.—*St. Matth.*, v, 16.

According to the recommendation of the Apostle, Religious should ever strive to be a means of edification to all who come in contact with them, by their modesty, their charity, their kindness, and the urbanity of manners which all expect from them.

The Bishops must be the first object of their greatest respect; next, the Priests, of whom they will ever speak with proper reverence. Let the Congregation of the Holy Cross deserve to be set down as exemplary in conduct and sentiments towards the Sacred Hierarchy of the Church.

Should they ever hear of any divisions in a Diocese or in a parish, they will stand aloof, and try to conciliate minds and hearts in all charity to Ecclesiastical authority.

The Religious of the Holy Cross should be polite to all men, and show contempt to none, especially among the poor, or the ignorant, or the sick.

Their intercourse with persons of the world should always be justified by charity, necessity, or strict requirements of society.

In all their dealings with the world, they will be just, honest, truthful—and never mean, small, or crooked.

They shall not unnecessarily multiply their visits or correspondence with anyone outside; much less with persons of another sex. Except in colleges, where parents are wont to be invited to meals, no stranger or friend shall be thus entertained in our Religious Houses. Religious mixing with the world are soon drawn to the world instead of drawing the world to themselves.

RULE XXXVII.

Of Epistolary Correspondence.

I had many things to write unto thee: but I would not by ink and pen write to thee. But I hope speedily to see thee, and we will speak mouth to mouth. Peace be to thee. Our friends salute thee. Salute the friends by name.—3 *Epist. St. John*, i, 13, 14.

Happy are those who, being obliged to carry on correspondence with others, know like Saint John how to do it for the edification of those they address, and never waste their time uselessly.

In a House of fifty Religious or more, as well as in one of two or three, the correspondence wholly passes through the hands of the Superior or the Director, whose privilege, and not unfrequently duty, it is to open all letters excepting those from or to higher authorities in the Congregation. No one has a right to mail a letter or take one from the post-office, nor should be permitted to do it. The watching over the correspondence of a House is one of the duties of its head. Any violation of this Rule, or attempt to establish a secret correspondence, is visited in all Communities with severe punishment.

If anyone has a reasonable motive to write or receive a letter unopen, let him apply for leave to the Superior, who will grant it if it is justified.

This being a universal custom in all Religious

Orders, to set it aside would show no Religious disposition in subjects, while it would be an insult to the Superior.

Here is the rule for all—viz.: Every Religious hands his letters *unsealed* to his Superior or Director, and receives from him alone his correspondence, OPEN.

No communication or controversy can be sent to newspapers without a special leave from the Provincial, except in case of visible and urgent necessity.

Letters of Direction may sometimes be allowed by the Superior to pass unopen; but even then only for a short time.

Should anyone write anything derogatory to the character of a House or of a member of the Congregation, unless justified in so doing by his position or duty,—viz.: fulfilling a monitor's obligations, &c., he ought to be severely punished for the offence: for any member whose mind is not religious will diffuse outside by his letters the poison of his diseased heart, than which nothing can be more detrimental to union, charity, and obedience. Words fly, but writings remain: circumstances, persons even, change, and what has been written unguardedly is some time afterwards brought out with a crushing weight.

Whoever would dare to stop or open a correspondence with superior officers would grievously violate his vow of obedience.

The initials S. N. D. B., "Praised be the name of the Lord," are first written at the head of each letter.

RULE XXXVIII.

Of Visits and Journeys.

You are not of the world.—*St. John*, xv, 19.

Separated as they are by Religious vows from the world, the Religious of the Holy Cross destined to preach or to teach will have to make and receive visits, to travel and mix more or less with the world. Hence the obligation on their part, after the example of Jesus and His Apostles, to be in the world without being of the world.

No one shall be permitted to visit, without necessity, persons of another sex, especially Religious, or to receive their visits except in common parlors.

Let every Religious respect himself, and always keep himself above suspicion.

All visits commanded by usage, common sense or charity should be made.

The Superior General should not travel alone; and, as much as possible, the Provincials also should be accompanied by a member of the Congregation. Indeed it is not the spirit of the Church that Religious should ever go out alone.

Before going on a journey, and on returning, every Religious shall pay a visit to the Blessed Sacrament and ask the blessing of his Superior if the Superior is a Priest. He shall also ask the blessing of the Superior when visiting him in his room for the first time in the morning or the last time in the evening.

A special leave is necessary to justify the absence of any Religious for the night. In case the absence should be protracted beyond three days, the Provincial's permission is required, unless the nature of a duty or obedience dictates it.

Travelling to a different Province is permitted only by the Superior General. At all events no Religious should leave his Community for any length of time, or be received in any other House of the Congregation, without a due written permission from his Superior.

True Religious rarely ask to go and visit their relatives in the world; they leave their regular Houses only when sent on some errand, and return as soon as the object of their journey is accomplished.

No one should leave his post to visit the higher officers without being expressly permitted to do so.

A Religious cannot change his Province for another without the mutual consent of the two Provincials and the sanction of the Superior General.

When a Religious sets out for a journey of any length he recites from his *Directory* the prayers of the "Itinerary."

When Superiors allow a journey, they supply the means to perform it decently and economically.

If a Religious changes his residence, or is sent on Mission, he takes with him what is marked by the Rule, and the Steward sees to it in person.

Whenever a member of the Congregation spends some days in a House of the Community he shall scrupulously follow the rules of the House until he leaves it.

The first visit should always be made to the Blessed Sacrament; and the last also.

The hospitality of any friend or acquaintance should never be preferred to that of the Congregation itself.

RULE XXXIX.

Of the Annual Retreat.

Come apart into a desert place.—*St. Mark*, vi, 31.

In compliance with the above sacred invitation, the members of the Congregation in each Province shall assemble yearly at the Provincial residence, to perform together the salutary exercises of a General Retreat.

As much as practicable, this Annual Retreat should open on the 8th of August and close on Assumption day.

An efficient preacher must be procured for the occasion, and measures are taken in order to secure complete peace and freedom from exterior cares to all engaged in the exercises. Perfect silence exists throughout, and no conversation whatever is allowed anywhere on the premises.

One of the best readers occupies the stand at all the meals.

In the Refectory, practices of humility and mortification are continued to the end. All wait, in turn, on the tables.

Every morning the chief Director of work reads out a list of names for the various employments of the place, and each one endeavors scrupulously to fulfil his task.

The Mass and Communions are suspended, and all prepare for a good review of the entire year.

On Assumption day the vows are renewed, Professions are made, the holy habit is given, and obediences are distributed.

RULE XI.

Of Vacations.

Jesus therefore being wearied with His journey, sat thus on the well.—*St. John*, iv, 6.

God in His justice might have exacted from us a constant application, and an unceasing labor; but in His mercy He deigns to care for our weakness; and in the same manner as He has given our senses a time for repose, He likewise grants us a little rest from our fatigues. The words of the above text justify it by the example of Jesus Himself.

The teaching members are allowed to take yearly some vacation, for a month or two; but they must bear in mind that vacations should be sanctified by the same practices of piety as the rest of the year; they should even show a greater care, being then more exposed to danger.

The Little Office of the Blessed Virgin is daily recited by everyone without exception, unless properly dispensed.

Three hours in the forenoon are employed in regular and graded classes, in such a manner as sensibly and materially to benefit every teacher according to his needs.

Properly speaking, the afternoons constitute the time of rest for vacations.

All the members of the same Province spend

the vacation months in the same place, together, and in due time attend there the exercises of the General Retreat. The privilege of returning thus, yearly, to the central House, should be refused only when it is absolutely impossible to allow it.

RULE XLI.

Of the Care of the Aged and of the Sick.

I was sick, and you visited Me.—*St. Matth.*, xxv, 36.

Jesus Christ looks upon what is done to sick persons as though it were done to Himself: hence the tender care which faith secures to the aged members, who have consumed their lives in the service of the Congregation, and to those who are tried by sickness in it.

Let the ancients be honored by all; let the infirm be soothed with all possible tenderness in their infirmities.

Superiors will consider it one of their first duties, in their daily visits to the sick, to see that they receive by day and by night every attention and relief which can be dictated by an unfeigned charity, a sympathizing meekness, and a solicitude of the heart. Medical prescriptions must be scrupulously and intelligently executed.

On their part, the sick Religious will accept their sufferings in a spirit of faith, and bear them with patience and resignation, in close union with Jesus Christ suffering and dying; and in order to fortify themselves in these dispositions, and derive from their sickness a greater merit, they will receive the Sacraments as often, if possible, as they were wont to do when in health and in strength.

Sickness tests virtue, and shows what there is in a man. Oh! what an edification is found by the sick bed of a fervent Religious! But, alas, how distressing is the sight of one whose thoughts and sentiments and views and habits were rather those of a worldly man than of a Religious! Here is a subject of meditation for all.

As soon as any serious danger is anticipated, greater zeal must be exercised to prepare the soul for the awful passage to eternity, and console it in its last moments. The last Sacraments are administered in time, in the presence of the Community, and the prayers for the agonizing are recited before the dying has lost his faculties and senses.

When the agony has commenced, the members of the House are again summoned around the sick bed, that all may assist the dying with their fervent prayers, and learn themselves how to live in order to die well. If God restores the sick person to health, he gradually resumes his pious exercises as soon as practicable.

RULE XLII.

Of the Duties towards the Deceased Members of the Congregation, and of certain Indulgences.

It is therefore a holy and wholesome thought to pray for the dead, that they may be loosed from sins.—*II Mach.*, xii, 46.

As soon as the soul has departed, the Community recite the prayers prescribed in the *Directory*, and the Superior of the House closes the eyes of the deceased member, and from this moment until the hour of burial two Religious recite continually by the corpse the Office of the Dead.

Immediately—or as soon as convenient—the death is announced by the tolling of the bell; the body is washed, and clothed with the Religious habit; then it is laid in the coffin, without any covering on the face unless it be too much altered by death; the hands are joined on the breast, as in the attitude of prayer, and the formula of the vows is placed in their hold.

The following day, at the appointed time, the

body is carried in procession to the Church and thence to the cemetery, accompanied by all the Religious of the House.

Immediately before letting it down into the earth, the Superior covers the face of the deceased and closes the coffin.

On the tomb is erected a simple wooden cross, painted in black, and upon it are written the name in religion and the family name of the deceased with the dates of his birth, Profession and death.

Under the same heading and dates there shall be inscribed an obituary of the deceased in a book exclusively dedicated to perpetuate the memory of the dead, and from which the same shall be read out annually, before the *Martyrology*, on the anniversary of the death. Without delay, the Superior informs the Provincial of the death, that he may announce the same to the Superior General, with request to solicit the suffrages of the Congregation for the departed soul. The suffrages range as follows:

For a Novice: one low Mass at the place where he dies, and a general Communion in the Novitiate, with the Beads and the Way of the Cross.

For a Novice having made temporary vows: a solemn Mass where he dies, with a Communion, the Way of the Cross and the Beads from each member of the Congregation.

For a Professed: a solemn service for the burial, and another on the seventh day thereafter, both with one nocturn only, at the place of his death: all the priests of the Congregation offer one Mass, and the other Religious one Communion, the Way of the Cross and the Beads.

For a Local Superior: besides a Mass from each Priest of the Congregation the two aforesaid services are celebrated, with three nocturns, at the place of burial.

For a Provincial or a General Functionary there is added an anniversary solemn service at the place of burial. For any of the above Superiors, all the Religious offer two Communions, and the Way of the Cross and the Beads twice each. Furthermore, for a Provincial, each House of the Province offers two low Masses; for a General Functionary each House of the Congregation offers three Masses.

The Superior General has a right to three complete services and an anniversary in the Mother House; to three low Masses from each Priest; to three Communions, three times the Way of the Cross and Beads from each Religious, and finally to the Community Mass for six months.

Every Religious who hears of the death of his father or mother has a right to solicit one Mass.

At the beginning of the year each Priest says

one Mass for the Superior General and his Assistants, and another for all the functionaries of the Congregation and its living benefactors. At the close of a Chapter, whether General or Provincial, a solemn Mass is celebrated for all the deceased benefactors of the Congregation.

There is a community of prayers and spiritual interests between the Sisters of the Holy Cross and this Congregation, and therefore a mutual reciprocity of suffrages for the dead.

The various Indulgences especially granted to the Congregation are yearly published in the *Ordo*, as they are renewed or increased by the Holy See.

Among the precious consolations which a Community life offers to a Religious soul, there is perhaps none calculated to make a deeper impression than the suffrages above described. In the world, the adage "Out of sight out of mind" is unfortunately too true. In Religion, the memory of the dear dead is vividly and sweetly kept in the hearts of the pious survivors; and in truth the fervor of a Congregation is nowise better attested than by its undying and prayerful affection for its departed members.

RULE XLIV.

Of Elections.

He went out into a mountain to pray, ... And when day was come, He called His disciples; and He chose twelve of them.—*St. Luke*, vi, 12, 13.

The election here treated of is the choice made by the General Chapter, of Religious to fulfil certain offices of the Congregation; the choice is always made by ballot, and the assembled voters or electors choose two of their number to count the votes and make known the result.

The voting is by secret ballot, and the plurality of votes decides the election, except in case of the Superior General, for whose election a two-third vote is required; the president takes an active part in all elections, but in case of a tie he is not allowed a casting vote; the decision in such a case must be referred to the next higher authority: that is, the local Superior refers to the Provincial, the Provincial to the Superior General, and the Superior General to the Congregation of the Propaganda.

However, the number of votes for and against must be made known when the *Constitution* requires either a plurality, as in the case of elections in general, or a two-third vote, as in the case of dismissal of Professed members. But silence should be observed in regard to the election of the Superior General, and nothing more is done than to make known the election when any member receives a sufficient number of votes.

No functionary canonically elected may refuse the charge with which he is invested, nor resign it without the consent of the Chapter: and to obtain such consent a plurality of votes must be had, as in the elections.

Before all other proceedings, the president must appoint a secretary to write the minutes of the commencement of the meeting, and two scrutators to count the votes, the president always being a scrutator *de jure*. These provisional officers cede their places to those who shall afterwards be elected.

When a Superior General is to be chosen, the election is preceded by one hour's prayer in the Chapter room. For other elections, only a quarter of an hour's prayer is made. Moreover, during the election of a Superior General no elector is allowed to go out; nor anyone of the House, without indispensable need; but the whole Community must observe silence, fast that day, and so arrange that, until the election takes place, as many Masses as possible be said at the high altar, that Communions be made, and the Way of the Cross performed by as many as can and as often as possible.

The electors shall take advantage of the afternoon preceding the day of the election, from two o'clock until Spiritual Reading, to confer together concerning those who may seem the best qualified for the General Superiorship, in order to make, in Chapter, immediately before the election, the catalogue of those eligible to the office, and to strike out the names of those who, in the opinion of all, are incapable of fulfilling such a charge, or who may have sought it. But, after taking such information, under the seal of secrecy, no one is allowed to be interrogated, either before or during the time of the election; and when asking information, all shall studiously avoid saying or asking for whom they shall vote.

The first Assistant shall have previously designated an elector to make an exhortation upon the election, which should have been submitted to his approval, and should contain no personal allusions to eligible members, but simply state the qualities required for the Superiorship, and insist on purity of intention in a vote of such importance, and upon the exclusion of all those who had sought the office.

Early on the morning of the election, the first Assistant shall sing the Mass *de Spiritu Sancto*, at which all the electors, whether Priests or not, shall Communicate, and after Mass the electors are conducted to the Chapter-room in procession by the Community, singing the *Veni Creator*, and as soon as they enter the door is closed.

This Rule is then read, after which a secretary

and two scrutators are elected, and they take the following oath:

I, ..., take God, who has caused me to be chosen Secretary, as my witness that I will faithfully fulfil all the obligations of my charge, and will do so with the most loyal intentions. In the name of the Father, and of the Son, and of the Holy Ghost. Amen.

I, ..., take God, before whom nothing is hidden, as my witness that I will act in good faith, without fraud or trickery, in my office of Scrutator, and will keep as much as is necessary the secrecy in regard to the voting. In the name of the Father, and of the Son, and of the Holy Ghost. Amen.

The secretary and two scrutators just elected shall then take the place of those who had been appointed provisionally, after the retiring secretary shall have written the minutes in regard to their elections.

Each of the electors takes the following oath:

I, ..., promise to God and to the Congregation never to reveal anything that is discussed in this Chapter, and to consult only my own conscience in the examination of affairs submitted to me for my consideration, nor will I ask or receive advice from anyone, except by way of information. Moreover I promise to do my utmost for the success of the affairs submitted to the consideration of the

Chapter. In the name of the Father, and of the Son, and of the Holy Ghost.

The assembly answer: *Amen.*

The one who is to deliver the discourse upon the election asks the blessing of the president—except in the case that the preacher be a Bishop not a member of the Congregation—goes into the pulpit and delivers his discourse.

Then all the electors make their accusation in Chapter, the president first, and then all the others by the lips of one who makes the accusation in the name of all; and, immediately after, the president pronounces the following absolution:

Ego, ..., Superior Generalis (Primus Assistens) Congregationis à Sâ. Cruce ...., auctoritate Dei omnipotentis, mihi, licet indignissimo, concessâ, vos absolvo à quibuslibet sententiis, pœnis et impedimentis in nostrâ Congregatione contra vos latis, et, quantum sit opus, dispenso vobiscum super quovis defectu ad hoc Capitulum pertinente, ut, si quâ sententiâ, pœnâ, vel quolibet impedimento nunc innodati estis, ob defectum aliquem in electionibus vel deliberationibus præcedentibus, nullâ ratione Capitulantibus hic congregatis id itâ noceat, ut legitimi non censeantur ipsorum actus. ✠ *In nomine Patris, et Filii, et Spiritus Sancti.*

The assembly respond: *Amen.*

The president declares the Chapter constitutionally formed, and each member takes the following oath of union:

I, ..., promise to God and to the Congregation never to say or do, or to allow to be said or done, anything which might occasion or favor division between the two Societies, unless the Holy See judge otherwise; and should I prove unfaithful to my oath in a culpable manner, I consent to be deprived of all offices and vote in Chapter. In the name of the Father, and of the Son, and of the Holy Ghost.

The assembly responds: *Amen.*

The president intones: *Deus in adjutorium meum intende*, and *Gloria Patri*, etc.; then, kneeling, he recites the following prayer:

Behold us, O God, assembled together in Thy name, to second the designs of Thy Providence upon the Work Thou hast deigned to confide to us, but trembling with the fear of hindering the accomplishment of Thy desires—for sin has filled our minds with darkness, and our hearts with perverseness. Come, then, in our midst; preside over this assembly; suggest to us what we should think, say and do: permit us not to forget in our deliberations the respect due to authority, and that charity which should unite all the members of the same family; and, above all, grant us the grace of having nothing in view but Thy greater glory, our own sanctification and the edification of our brethren.

The assembly respond: *Amen.*

Before proceeding to the elections, each elector takes the following oath:

I, ..., take God, who hears me, as my witness that I shall cast my vote for Superior General (Assistant) in favor of him whom in my soul and conscience I believe most worthy of the charge. In the name of the Father, and of the Son, and of the Holy Ghost.

All respond: *Amen.*

When any member shall have obtained one more than the half of all the votes, or, in case of the election of the Superior General, two-thirds of all the votes, the President simply declares the election made, except in the case of the election of the Superior General or of the General Procurator, when the election is announced by the following decree:

The vote of the Chapter, legitimately constituted, having designated for Superior General (Procurator General) the Rev. Father ...., I, ..., by the authority of the Holy See and of the Congregation, declare the Rev. Father .... Superior General (Procurator General) of the Congregation of the Holy Cross, provided His Holiness, the Pope, confirms the election. In the name of the Father, and of the Son, and of the Holy Ghost. Amen.

He then signs the decree and affixes the seal of the Congregation.

The seal shall consist of a Cross to which shall be affixed two anchors. The *exerque* bears the words, *Congreg. a Sa. Cruce*, and under the Cross the words *Spes unica.* The seal of individual Houses should have, besides, the name of the locality; for instance: *Capit. Prov. Gall. Congreg. a Sa. Cruce.*

If the president be elected, the secretary writes and signs the decree. If the election be prolonged, the electors should go without breakfast and recreation.

The one elected cannot refuse the charge, and in the case of the General Superiorship he falls on his knees, kisses the ground, arises and awaits in silence the confirmation of the Holy Father, all the electors being obliged to keep inviolable the secret until such confirmation be had.

The election of a Superior General or of a Procurator General shall not be published until after it has been submitted to the Cardinal Prefect of the Propaganda, and by His Eminence to the Holy Father.

RULE XLV.

Of Foundations.

Unless the Lord build the house, they labor in vain that build it.—*Ps.* cxxvi, 1.

No new Establishment should be undertaken without a suitable number of proper subjects and a security of reasonable means of existence and and success.

For a new foundation of great importance, the sanction of the Holy See is required.

Every new foundation must rest on a written contract, well digested, and signed by all contracting parties, on three copies: the first, for the authorities of the place, the second, for the Superior or Director of the House, and the third for the Provincial.

As much as practicable, new Establishments should not be made too far from some other Houses of the Congregation, on the principle that scattered and isolated Houses have not the same chances of success, and still less the same guarantees to continue in Religious dispositions.

No foundation should be accepted for one member alone: our blessed Lord sent His disciples two by two.

Before subjects are sent to a new foundation, a Visitor should always go and ascertain if all is ready that is required by the Rule.

An exact inventory of what is found in the Establishment is drawn up and preserved with care.

Whenever it is possible, the travelling expenses of the first subjects should be paid by those who have obtained the foundation.

RULE XLVI.

Of Superiors, Directors and Assistant Teachers.

Constitution XVI states that the heads of Establishments shall receive the title of Superiors or Directors according to the importance of said Houses. In ordinary cases the Superior General will name *Superior* any Religious at the head of three other Religious, provided he is a Professed member and has given proofs of devotedness to the Congregation; that he has shown himself previously a man of order and economy, and, above all, a man of discipline and regularity.

When a Religious receives the title of Superior, he solicits from the Provincial the formation of a Council, if there is none yet in the House, in order to avoid any irregular and unconstitutional act in administering the affairs of the Establishment.

All Superiors being by right members of the Provincial Chapter, are bound to assist thereat; if prevented by sickness or other cause, they should be represented therein by the Assistant or some other Professed from among the best qualified.

In all Houses of less than four Religious, the title of *Director* is given to the head of the Establishment.

The Superiors and Directors shall hold with the Provincial the same intercourse which the latter holds with the Superior General, with the restrictions specified in the *Constitutions* and the *Rules*. Inasmuch as they share more or less in the government of the Congregation, it is their duty to respect and love the higher Administration and see the same respected and loved everywhere in the Congregation. They forward their quarterly statistics and write to their Provincial in a religious and business-like manner. Any neglect on this point proves that there is a wrong man in the wrong place.

If they have to propose a Novice for Profession they give the Provincial all the information required by the Rule on the admission to vows.

They must be deeply convinced that a Superior or Director is so appointed not to be served, but rather to serve, and minister unto others. The head of a House must see to all its wants, not in a general way, but in detail; he must make himself all to all,—aiding the weak and assisting those in trial and temptation; he must be the man of God, and of all under his charge; he must be ready to forget himself and his own ease and comfort and liberty, in order to be, at all times, the benefactor, the generous friend and efficient helper of all around him.

Superiors and Directors, above all, must give to the Community an unfeigned and constant example of fidelity to spiritual exercises and to the Rules; they must maintain discipline, take measures to secure the same on the part of each and of all in the House they govern, preserve peace and harmony among all, attend to the wants of soul and body from the first to the last,

If the Superior is a Priest, everyone visiting him in the morning or at night, in his room, kneels for his blessing, in the same manner as he would to the Provincial himself.

They must procure an extraordinary Confessor for the House every Ember Week.

They visit at least once a week the various departments of the House, and every room in it, to ascertain if everything is in order; from time to time they likewise carefully examine everything in the church or chapel, in the vestry, the library, the archives, etc.

With regard to the temporal administration, all Superiors scrupulously follow in this important portion of the government the rule and method adopted by the Provincial Chapter, especially in what concerns the stewardship, the keeping of the books, &c.

Superiors of educational Establishments must apply themselves to the forming of good teachers, always preferring Religious to seculars, and Priests to laymen. They must continually watch them, and encourage or praise, reprove or stir them up as they may deserve or require.

No blame, however, or censure, should ever be administered to them before the children; for their teaching, their authority and their influence should be upheld and carefully preserved to the last. As long as they do their duty well, they must be assured of the satisfaction they give, of the high esteem in which the Superior holds them, of the confidence reposed in them, and of the kind feelings entertained for them. Hence the mutual affection and reliance which give efficacy to teaching and a peculiar charm to living in such Houses.

Several times a week all the teachers should be assembled to receive some explanations of their duties, some advice on their manner of acting in the class-room, and such new directions as time and circumstances may require.

On Saturday they present their notes for the week ending, and the president makes his general remarks on the present state of the school, with the view to check or stop what might prove dangerous and to encourage whatever is best calculated to promote the good of the institution.

Superiors must have a fatherly care of the sick in their Houses.

In boarding Houses the Superiors themselves preside at the spiritual reading of the pupils, in order to give them all the advice they may need on religious behavior, on discipline, on studies, cleanliness, politeness, health, letter-writing, economy, their duty to God, to their parents, to their professors, &c., &c., &c. They also preside at the public reading of the notes on Saturdays. They see that a Retreat of a few days be given to the pupils, yearly. They pay serious attention to the preparation of all classes for an earnest examination.

The Superior, if a Priest, celebrates Mass every morning in the presence of the Community and the pupils, and presides at all the religious exercises. He alone corresponds with the boarders' parents or guardians. He reads attentively all notes and bulletins before they are sent out, as some of them may require modification or annotation by himself.

Superiors must be perfectly posted on every point of the regulations, on the plan of studies, on all programmes for examinations, public exercises, &c. Nothing should be done in their Houses without their knowledge and sanction.

It is scarcely necessary to add that however

zealous and devoted a Superior may be, he will still never accomplish anything unless thoroughly assisted by efficient, obedient and able Religious.

RULE XLVII.

Of the Missioners.

Quam speciosi pedes evangelizantium pacem, evangelizantium bona!

Of all the offices to which a Priest of the Holy Cross can be appointed, that of a Missioner, who is directly charged to preach the Gospel to people extraordinarily assembled to listen to the word of God, and devote unusual attention to the great affair of their salvation, stands first in importance and gravity, and alike requires more than any other the virtues and abilities which, when blended together in a conspicuous degree, make a Religious a model of obedience and humility, of zeal and piety, of devotedness and fervor. To be a real Missioner, one should be a Saint; a man of prayer and regularity; a priest of God, and not a man of this world; a man dead to self and profoundly alive to the responsibilities of his sublime minis try.

From the first moment he arrives at the place of

his destination, until he leaves it, he must be, and appear to be, as one sent by God, whose countenance and every act and word should edify, and be remembered for years after.

If he realizes at all the nature and the greatness of the task entrusted to his hands, he will spare no pains to carry it out, and yet will deem all his efforts as mere sounding brass unless God Himself blesses them with the abundance of His graces.

Let no Superior entertain the thought of making an efficient Missioner out of a Priest not deeply imbued with the spirit of faith and humility, or of one who is self-conceited and not exemplary in obeying orders and following a direction lawfully given. God will not bless the proud or worldly-minded preacher; and if a Mission is not blessed from heaven it will be worse than nothing. Hence the propriety of commending every new Mission to the prayers and Communions of fervent Communities.

No Missioner should ever take upon himself to accept or promise a Mission; it is the exclusive and undelegated privilege of the Provincial or Vicar. Except on short Missions of a week, or triduos preparatory to a First Communion or a Confirmation, no Missioner is sent alone; there must be at least two, after the example of the disciples sent out by Jesus Christ Himself. There is always one appointed Superior of the little band, and upon him alone devolves the duty to organize the order of the exercises, after a clear explanation with the Parish Priest or Pastor, whose unreserved adherence to the entire programme must be had.

Before a Missioner starts for a new Mission, he solicits his Provincial's special blessing upon himself and the exercises he is about to open, and with him he makes sure of the prayers of the Community for his success. Then he visits the Blessed Sacrament for the same purpose. As soon as he can find it convenient on his way he devoutly recites the prayers of the *Itinerary*, and from that moment until he reaches his destination he tries to keep his mind fixed on the great task before him. His recollected and composed manner already begins to preach and to edify. Has he not cause for serious reflections?

When arrived at the place of the Mission he salutes the Pastor, and, begging his or the Bishop's blessing, before going to his room he asks to be conducted to the church, where, for a few moments, he earnestly commends to our Blessed Lord the Mission, which, in His merciful designs, is to work such a change in many a soul.

He then avails himself of the first opportunity to have an interview with the Pastor, to assure him, first of all, of his unfeigned desire to serve him to the best of his ability, and then to obtain from him all the information he may deem proper to communicate on the religious state of his people, on their best and their worst features, that he may know at once where he stands and on what to bear, etc.

The programme of the exercises once agreed upon, they both, the Missioner and the Pastor, return before the Blessed Sacrament, place the written page on the altar and pray awhile for the Divine blessing. From this moment the Pastor must be convinced, and remain convinced, that a man of God has come to help him. Then they go to visit the Religious Communities, if there are any in the place, to beg of them special prayers for the success of the Mission.

As long as the Mission continues, the Missioner shows himself a model of regularity, both for his own religious exercises and for the public services of the programme.

The exercises once closed, the Missioners leave the place and follow the direction given them.

On all occasions they try to travel with economy, make no purchases unnecessarily without due leave, and forward to the Provincial a report of the Mission together with the amount they have received for their labors. Let them bear in mind the obligations of their vows, lest after preaching to others they may themselves be lost. There can be no doubt that great dangers encompass such labors; but if the vows are strictly kept, they will keep all safe, and God's grace will follow.

Whoever has been appointed Superior of the Missioners, or even of a Mission, must see that his assistants are supplied with healthy rooms and food, etc., as also that they lead with him a religious life; allowing none to work beyond his strength, but distributing the labors of the Mission with discriminative intelligence, and in fact, trying to preserve both the health and fervor of his little band.

Missions are fields which should yield, under a wise management, rich harvests of postulants, pupils, subscribers to the Ave Maria, and friends to the Congregation.

Once more let it be understood that our Missioners are not allowed to undertake anything of importance on Missions without the Pastor's consent, and still less to meddle, in any way, with ecclesiastical appointments or changes. They must be extremely cautious, and prudent, and reserved, in relating anything of what they may have noticed or heard, even to their Superiors or to the Ordinary, from the fact that a Missioner is, first of all, a Confessor in the eyes of the people, and that, therefore, any suggestion from him to ecclesiastical authority, bears, *prima facie*, the appearance of a revelation of Confession.

Wherever a zealous, able and prudent Missioner shall have given a Mission, Pastor and people will always bless the day he came among them; both shall have been equally edified, benefited, made better, and will hold his memory in grateful love.

Unless for peculiar or local reasons some modifications be deemed necessary, the following is the plan which our Missioners adopt, viz.:

At 6 A. M.—Meditation, or a plain explanation of Christian duties.

6.30 A. M.—First Mass; second at 8 30.

9 A. M.—Sermon, for one hour.

7 P. M.—Sermon, for one hour.

After this, Benediction of the Blessed Sacrament.

Between the Sermons.—Confessions, etc.

Wherever Religious Confraternities exist, they are assembled in turn at a convenient hour, say 2 o'clock P. M., and addressed as such.

No Sermon lasts over an hour.

At 9 and 7 the Sermons are always preceded by some pious singing.

The Plenary Indulgence to be gained is announced at the opening of the exercises.

The natural order of Sermons is: The importance of salvation; the great subjects of death, judgment, hell, eternity; the Passion and death of our Saviour; then the Church, Confession, Communion, Holy Mass, Priesthood, devotedness to our Holy Faith; duties of Catholic parents to secure a Catholic education to their children; dangers to be avoided, means of preservation; devotion to the Blessed Virgin Mary; prayer; frequent reception of the Sacraments; pious associations; good readings; liberality towards the support of the Church and Pastor.

A worthy Missioner thinks more of the salvation of souls than of the salary which mercenaries seek for their services. If the Mission proves a success, a deep gratitude will attest it exteriorly. If the people give little, perhaps they give even more than they were obliged; in a Mission which everyone knows to be a failure, what remuneration can be expected?

At the close of a successful Mission, the Missioner announces that whatever he will receive will go, after his own travelling expenses are paid, towards the object his Provincial shall have named yearly.

Then, with the Pastor's sanction, a public lecture may be delivered by the Missioner, its proceeds to be divided equally between the Pastor and the lecturer.

During the Mission, the Missioner lives as much as possible retired in his room, and carefully avoids all manner of levity, even at table. He should not stay long in recreation after meals.

The Pastor should remain edified, raised in his people's esteem, and a friend to the Congregation.

RULE XLVIII.

Of Manual Labor in general, and of some Particular Employments in this Department.

In a Religious Congregation there is no mean employment; whatever is done in a spirit of faith, in the service of God, is noble, on account of the object in view. It is not the office that ennobles a man, but personal merit that ennobles the office.

The Brothers named Directors of employments shall have all the implements necessary to their work, with a proper inventory of the same.

Every year the various inventories are closely examined by the Superior or the Steward, in presence of both the one who leaves the employment and the other who enters upon it. This usually takes place at the General Retreat. Each succeeding year should show a due increase of order and economy.

The Directors of employments are alone responsible to the Administration for the trust, whatever its importance may be. But, in justice, the Administration must secure to them a reasonable number of hands, willing to work and to follow the direction of the head man.

One of the first duties of these Directors is to form the men given them to the employment they are to fulfil: they must be patient with them; but they must carefully watch them, until they know thoroughly how to discharge their obedience. Above all, the aids must find in their Directors the example of a Religious life.

On Sunday there shall be a meeting of all the Directors of employments, presided over by the Steward or the Superior himself. In this meeting every Director reports, and shows what has been done during the week in his own department; he states the dispositions of his *employés*, the difficulties met with, the advantages that could be obtained, and what remains to be done the following week. Such regular meetings, if properly conducted, must necessarily secure valuable amendments and facilitate the task of all the Religious concerned. If the president is satisfied that any measure carried by the majority would prove detrimental, he suspends it until the Superior has decided the question.

Of the Infirmarian.—The Infirmarians should be noted for their mildness, patience, firmness, foresight, vigilance, and compassion for the sufferings of others—beholding Jesus in the persons of the sick, in order to be more attentive to their needs and to render them cheerfully the services most repugnant to nature.

They shall acquit themselves of their employment with that solicitude which is expected of them, not only by the Congregation, to which they have devoted their life, but also by the students, and the parents who have confided their children to the institution, and who depend upon the Infirmarians that proper care be given them in case of sickness.

They shall constantly keep the apartments of the infirmary scrupulously clean, neat and tidy, placing pious pictures on the walls, and putting flowers in the rooms according as the season and the physician may permit; remove everything from the sick that may exhale a bad odor; take care that the beds be made at least once a day, and that the sheets, &c., be frequently changed, so as to preserve the greatest cleanliness and neatness. They shall never fail to accompany the physician when he visits the sick; to inscribe the visits on a register; to keep with them the prescriptions written and signed by the physician, and to write upon a special register all they buy for and furnish to the sick.

The Infirmarians shall receive no one without an order from the Prefect of Health, except in unforeseen and sudden cases, and then they shall immediately inform him of what has happened.

They shall never humor the whims of the sick to the detriment of the prescriptions of the physicians, and shall do all in their power to make the stay in the infirmary as little wearisome as possible,—taking a great care of the sick, foreseeing and forestalling all their reasonable wishes, taking them to walk out when convenient, and recreating them with agreeable conversation and pleasant and edifying reading.

If a student has to follow some particular *régime* without ceasing to attend class, the Infirmarians shall so arrange that the student be as little disturbed as possible from classes and study.

In case of dangerous sickness the Infirmarians shall inform the confessor and provide for the sick all the aids of religion.

If any students remain in bed in the morning in the college dormitory, the Infirmarian or the Prefect of Discipline shall see that an under-prefect be constantly in the dormitory. Every morning before breakfast and every evening before supper they shall place on the table of the Superior or Director of the House, or his substitute, the report of all the sick, mentioning their names and the state of each, having care to note in the column of observations whether, in case of one remaining in bed, it be in the infirmary or in the dormitory.

No noise is permitted in the infirmary; no visitors are admitted without special leave. The Doctor alone has a right to prescribe remedies. In Colleges there is always a special Prefect to preside in the convalescents' rooms and at their meals.

Cooks.—The Brother having charge of the kitchen shall prepare a wholesome, economical, and, at the same time, abundant nourishment for all, and at the same time shall vary the dishes as much as possible, without however using sugar, unless with the permission of the Superior.

He shall keep good order and neatness, recollection and silence in the kitchen, not, of course, an absolute silence, except from the Night Prayer until after Meditation next morning, but a silence that shall preclude all unnecessary and loud talk.

The helpers in the kitchen shall perform their duties in strict obedience to the chief cook or one whom he appoints.

REFECTORIANS AND CELLARISTS.—The Refectorians alone shall have the key of the refectories, to which they shall admit no one between meal times without the permission of the Steward.

They shall keep their refectories neat, in good order and well ventilated.

They shall take note of everything that is broken, in order to keep their inventory in good order. They shall also note the names of the students who break or damage anything in the refectory, and have the same charged to said students.

The waiters shall be ready in the refectory a sufficient time before meals to have everything prepared for the students or community. They shall be attentive to all the wants of those at the table which they wait upon.

The waiters must be polite, clean, prompt,

active, noiseless in their movements, never resting, anticipating every want, presenting, *to the left*, whatever is expected or asked, never taking too many dishes or plates at a time, breaking nothing, spilling or spoiling nothing.

They shall take their meals after the others, and shall make the Particular Examen at the first opportunity; if they have need of more help, they must apply in time to the Steward or Superior.

In places where they have charge of wine or liquors, they shall keep them under key, and never give away a bottle to anyone but on a written order from the Superior of the House. Everything in the cellar shall be arranged to the best advantage for the preservation of the wine, etc., in good condition. Especial care shall be taken that no wine spoil by not being bottled in time.

CHAMBERLAINS.—Those having charge of the rooms shall first find out at what hour they can make the rooms with the least inconvenience to the occupants; and shall take special care that the keys they have for opening doors do not fall into the hands of those who should not use them; they shall, moreover, take care to open only those doors they have a right to open. They should make the bed properly, not limiting their exertions to spreading the covers over the bed smoothly. They shall sweep the apartment, the corridors, stairways; dust the furniture, and wipe it some time after, when the dust shall have settled, and put the chairs, etc., in their proper place.

They shall also see that the body-linen, towels, etc., be changed, and that the soiled linen be taken to the wash-room.

They shall scrupulously avoid glancing at letters or papers which may have been left open or closed upon the table, or on the book-shelves, or in any part of the apartments.

An intelligent chamberlain may contribute immensely to the comfort and happiness of those whose rooms are intrusted to his charge. But it must be confessed that few men have even the first idea of the neatness in which a private room should be kept. To make up a room is not a great job; and yet, not one out of ten can do it properly. To sweep a room, for instance, should be different from raising the dust and spreading it over every piece of furniture. To empty a vessel properly, requires a thorough cleaning every time it is emptied. As to making a bed, a chamberlain will likely try his best, and will most probably succeed.

Dormitorians.—The Dormitorians are responsible for the order and cleanliness of the dormitories, the preservation of beds and bed-clothes.

In the morning they shall begin by thoroughly ventilating the dormitories and then airing the beds by throwing the bed-clothes to the foot of the bed; commencing at one end of the dormitory they turn down all quilts, etc., and recommence at the same end to make the beds. No bed should be made up until thus well aired. They should also take note when any bed-clothing has not the proper number or mark, and immediately inform the Steward and have the number or mark put on.

There is a chief Dormitorian, who is appointed to direct the work of all his assistants. He must see that each of them know to perfection how to discharge his office. In a week or two of assiduous teaching, every one can learn how to take care of a large dormitory. The work is done as early as possible; and when finished, but never before, the dormitory is open to visitors. No clothing, nor linen, nor boots or shoes, should be left on or under the beds. The floor must be swept perfectly clean; the room well ventillated; the spreads must tastefully cover each bed; the upper pillow-case must be kept unsoiled, and every care taken to give the room a striking appearance of neatness, comfort, and salubrity. The spreads are removed at night.

If they find any one in bed, sick, they shall at once inform the Prefect of Health, and take care not to open the windows so as to inconvenience the sick.

They shall collect the soiled body-linen, Sunday morning, and have it sent to the wash-room or carry it themselves, and shall take note of anything that may have been lost; they shall also change the sheets and pillow-cases the first Saturday of every month.

They shall follow the regulations of each Establishment in regard to the change of clothing during the week, and to the care of the clothing that has need of mending.

They shall pay especial attention to the ventilation of the dormitories during the day.

On Sundays and holidays of obligation the Steward shall have the Dormitorians assisted; and all who at that time are free shall consider it a matter of conscience to pay cheerful obedience to the call of the Steward, and thus enable their brothers to attend the religious Exercises of the day. Assistance should also be extended to those having charge of the wash-room, refectories, stables, &c.

THE CLOTHES-KEEPER.—The Clothes-keeper shall have charge of all the clothing, and attend to the mending thereof. He shall have a register, wherein he writes the list of all the clothing belonging to Professed, Novices, or Students; he shall mark all the clothing. He shall superintend the gathering up of the soiled linen, and see that it is taken to the Wash-room.

COMMON RULES.

CONSTITUTIONS

OF THE

CONGREGATION OF THE HOLY-CROSS.

CONSTITUTION I.

Ends of the Congregation of the Holy-Cross.

1. The Congregation of the Holy-Cross is composed of two societies, distinct but not separated, that is to say of priests or clergymen and lay brothers, who are divided into teaching and coadjutor brothers for the work of the different houses.

2. All are constituted according to the religious state by the simple vows of poverty, obedience and chastity under the name of Salvatorists and Josephites of the Holy-Cross.

3. The ends of the Congregation are as follows : 1. the perfection of individuals by

the practice of the evangelical counsels ; 2. the sanctification of one's fellow-creatures by the preaching of the word of God, especially in the country and foreign missions etc. ; 3. the Christian instruction and education of youth through the medium of schools in which letters and sciences are taught, and of schools of agriculture and of trades : these latter being especially destined to poor and abandoned children.

CONSTITUTION II.

Dependence on the Holy See.

4. The Congregation of the Holy-Cross will always be under the entire dependence of the holy See and the Sacred Congregation of the Propaganda.

5. The Superior General, elected by the General Chapter, will be confirmed by the holy See, and, once confirmed, will not be liable to be deposed by the General Chapter. The holy See alone will have the right to pronounce his dismissal.

6. Conformably to the Decree of Pius VII of the 22[d] August 1814, the Institute of the Holy-Cross will always have a house at Rome for the residence of its Procurator General near the holy See.

7. No new establishment can be founded without the permission of the Sacred Congregation of the Propaganda.

8. Every three years, after the closing of the General Chapter, the Superior General will lay before the sovereign Pontiff a report on the material and disciplinary state of the whole Institute.

9. The immoveable estates becoming the property of the Institute can only be alienated according to the canonical rules : nevertheless, it is permitted to the Superiors of the different houses to alienate to concurrence of the sum of one thousand francs. But if the interest of the Congregation require a more considerable alienation, the General will obtain the permission of the Bishop of the Diocese who, as apostolical delegate, may allow an alienation of five thousand francs :

any greater alienation can only be authorized but by the Holy See.

10. In the case of the suppression of the Institute, or the canonical separation of the two societies, all the moveable and immoveable estates will remain at the disposal of the Holy See, which in the last mentioned case, will judge, after cognizance of their origin, in what proportion the said estates ought to be divided.

11. The Congregation of the Holy-Cross professes, most particularly, to respect and obey the apostolical Constitutions and Decrees, the orders and counsels of the S. Congregation of the Propaganda, which has taken it under its protection.

CONSTITUTION III.

Dependence of the Congregation towards the Bishops of the Dioceses.

12. All the houses, all the establishments, of whatever nature they be, will depend on their respective Bishop, except in what re

gards the Constitutions, to which there cannot be brought any derogation.

13. In like manner, all the members of the Institute are bound to show obedience and respect to the diocesan Bishop in the limits prescribed by Benedict XIV in the apostolical Letters, *emanavit nuper*, of the 21st of January 1758, addressed to the Priests of S. Philip of Neri : that is to say, that the Congregation is subject to the Ordinary, except in whatever regards its Constitutions and other prescriptions expressly mentioned in the aforesaid apostolical Letters (Grand collection of the Bulls, vol. 19, pag. 23 of the appendix).

14. No Clergyman or Brother in the Institute can be admitted to the Novitiate without testimonial Letters from the Ordinary for the first, and from the proper curate for the Brothers.

15. The Clergymen of the Institute will receive the ordinations from the Bishop of the Diocese in which they reside.

16. All must have the sacred patrimony

and the dimissory Letters of their Ordinary.

17 Nevertheless the Holy apostolical See is humbly entreated to grant to the Congregation of the Holy Cross the Indult conceded by Benedict XIV, and by Leo XII in their apostolical Letters : *Inter religiosas familias*, addressed to the Liguorians, dated 24th March 1826 : that is to say, to be able to ordain the Clergymen under the plea of the common board empowering the Superior General to deliver them, himself, dimissory Letters conformably to the Brief already quoted of Leo XII. If those who should be thus ordained, happened to retire from the Congregation, they should regulate canonically their situation (1).

18. The Priests of the Institute must have the approbation of the Ordinary to be able to preach and hear the confessions of secular

(1) Quæ petitur venia, intelligitur facta ad decennium pro iis tantum casibus in quibus qui est ordinandus eo careat patrimonio quod de regula habere debet super quo superioris conscientia oneratur. (Extr. ex decreto.) approbat.

persons. Respecting the members of the Institute, the Holy apostolical See is humbly intreated to grant to the Congregation of the Holy Cross the privilege conceded to the missionary Priests by the apostolical Brief of Clement X, *Apostolici muneris*, dated July 10th 1671, and, by another Brief of Clement XI, *Pastoralis Officii*, of the 9th of January 1710, viz : that the Priests of the Institute, once approved for the confessions by the Ordinary of the Diocese in which they reside, may freely and with the permission only of the Superior General hear the confessions of the Religious of the Congregation in all the Houses of the Order.

19. The Ordinary has the right to visit the Houses personally, simultaneously with the Superior General or his delegate. Neither the Bishop nor the Superior General are empowered to annul the resolutions of each other; but in case of difference of opinion, they will arrange amicably the affair, and, if necessary, will have recourse to the Sacred Congregation of the Propaganda.

20. The General will, in no wise, be sub-

ject to the Bishops in the government of the Institute; but he shall deport himself towards them with all possible regards, conceding to them all he can, and maintaining with them a perfect understanding.

21. If the Bishop insists for the removal out of his Diocese of any Religious whatsoever, the General will take care to place elsewhere that Religious, and to substitute in his stead another subject agreable to the Bishop.

CONSTITUTION IV.

Means of the Congregation of the Holy Cross.

22. To attain its end, the Congregation of the Holy Cross forms its Members ; 1° to the religious life by the exercises of a Noviciate of a year at least and of two years at most; 2° to the apostleship by the predication of the word of God and the administration of the sacraments; to the teaching of Grammar, Letters, Sciences and various professions in the Seminaries, Colleges, Schools, Orphan's asylums and other charitable establishments.

23. The exercises of piety, whether they be special to the Novices or common to all, are determined by particular Rules, in order to establish, maintain and renew all and every one in the spirit of their holy calling: thus every day, Meditation, holy Mass, private Examination, spiritual Reading, visit to the most Blessed Sacrament and the recitation of Beads.

24. Every week coulps and Chapter, Confession, one hour of Adoration before the Blessed Sacrament, and Communion. The Holy Communion may also take place on Feast days.

25. Every month, one day's Retreat, Direction and Monition.

26. Every year, solemn Retreat; a few particular Feasts, especially that of the Sacred Heart of Jesus, Patronal of the Salvatorists; that of St. Joseph, Patronal of the Josephites, and that of the dedication of the Church of the Mother-House: the suffrages for the dead are also determined.

27. With respect to the material resour-

ces, the Congregation places its entire trust in God whose Providence, to this day, has taken care of all its wants and has already enriched it with real Estates both in France and in Foreign Countries.

CONSTITUTION V.

Admission of Candidates, their rights.

28. Nobody can be admitted to the Novitiate, without testimonial Letters, conformably to Constitution III. Nobody can be admitted to the emission of vows, if he has not previously had it in his power to become acquainted with this new mode of life, and all the duties which, it bears with it, during the time and according to the mode determined in the Constitutions on this matter.

29. Cannot be admitted those who are bound by the following impediments : marriage ; illegitimate birth ; expulsion from another Institute ; epilepsy or a contagious disease; defamation by a judicial sentence.

30. Every Candidate admitted must bring a determined suit of clothes, deposit or engage a sum assigned for the expenses of the Novitiate and studies. The pròrata of this sum will be returned to the owner in case he retires.

31. The Superior can dispense with the obligation of furnishing the above-mentioned sum.

32. Every Religious whether in health or in sickness has a right to a complete maintenance and to all the solicitude commanded by christian charity.

33. No Religious, after the emission of his vows can be dismissed save by the Superior General, with the two thirds of the voices of his counsel, for the offences determined in the present Constitutions, in which case is remitted to him, a suitable garment and the money necessary to return, either to his own family, or to the place from whence he started to go to the house which received him.

CONSTITUTION VI.

Of the Government of the Community.

34. The Congregation is governed by a Superior General aided by three assistant Salvatorists, and three assistant Josephites, who compose his counsel, and by a General Chapter.

35. The general dignitaries, besides the former, are : the Procurator, the Secretary, the Steward and the Treasurer General, all elected for six years and reeligible.

36. The particular dignitaries are : the Provincial, and previous to their definitive institution, the Vicars and their Assistants : the Stewards, Treasurers, Visitors, local Superiors, Masters of the Novices, Directors and Prefects, all named by an obedience of the General in his Council. The Procurator General near the Holy See and the local Superiors, as well as all the other dignitaries, save the General, may be chosen indifferently among the Salvatorists or the Josephites.

37. There is in the Mother-House a Steward General understood in this sense, not that all the goods of the Institute are common, but only the overplus of each house, of which the registers of the general Stewardship will make a special mention, in opening as many particular accounts.

CONSTITUTION VII.

Of the General Chapter.

38. The General Chapter is composed of the Superior General and his Assistants, the Procurator General near the Holy See, the Secretary, the Steward and the Treasurer General ; the Provincials and the Deputies of each Province for each triennium at the plurality of the suffrages, according to the number fixed by the General Chapter.

39. The number of the Salvatorists and Josephites will be the same in this Chapter. without comprising the President.

40. The number of the members of the

Chapter, first carried to twenty, may be successively augmented by the Chapter three years beforehand, according to circumstances.

41. The General Chapter has the right to assemble, every three years, at the Mother-House and may be convocated extraordinarily by the Superior General or him who is appointed in his stead, in the place mentioned in the Letter of convocation.

42. The General Chapter modifies, completes or abrogates every rule or disposition, emanated from its own authority; or from any other authority inferior to its own.

43. It elects by ballot the Superior General, the six Assistants, the Procurator, the Secretary, the Steward, and the Treasurer General; also the Provincials.

44. The Superior General is elected for life, the other dignitaries for six years. In order to avoid that all the elections be made the same year, the first time a part will take place for three years only.

45. It regulates the relations between the

different establishments; enacts on all difficulties occurring to them, gives its advice on the law-suits to be borne, if the time of its meeting allows it without detriment to the interests of the Institute.

46. It receives, discusses and approves all the accounts sent in by the Steward General.

47. It accepts, confirms or rejects the foundation of establishments which are proposed.

48. It emits advice on the erection of new provinces of the Institute, of houses of the Novitiate, and the Superior transmits this advice to the Holy See in asking for its erection.

49. It can, of its own authority, depose all the dignitaries, for one of the cases foreseen by the present Constitutions, except the Superior General.

50. If the case regarded the Superior General, the Chapter might be called together without the consent of the said Superior, by the

Assistants, on the demand of the majority of the members *de jure* of the Chapter, and the purport of the meeting would be made known in the letter of convocation.

51. In the Provincial or General Councils or Chapters, in case of division of the votes, the President has no casting vote, but the decision belongs to the respective Superior, so that, if in the Provincial Councils or Chapters, the votes are equally divided, the Provincial cannot decide; the affair is transmitted to the General, who, after previously taking advice of his Assistants, adopts such course as appears to him the surest and most reasonable; that if a similar difficulty produces itself in the General Chapter, the affair is sent over to the most Eminent Cardinal Prefect of the Propaganda who will take such resolution as will seem to him the most suitable to the circumstance.

CONSTITUTION VIII.

Of the Superior General.

52. The Superior General must be chosen among the professed priests, enjoying all the civil rights, aged thirty at least, members of the General Chapter, or at least among the local Superiors, professed since eight complete years.

53. He is elected for life by the General Chapter of the Congregation and confirmed by the Holy See.

54. He directs and administers the Congregation; he represents it, acts in its name before all jurisdictions, and unbinds the vows of poverty and obedience in the cases of exclusion foreseen by the Rules. No lawsuit can be taken up or instituted without his interference.

55. He attends to the observation of the Constitutions and Rules, to the preservation of good order, of discipline, and he exerts

all his efforts to diffuse a religious spirit among the members of the Congregation.

56. Therefore,all the members of the Society owe him respect, obedience and affection.

57. He signs and certifies all the acts of the Congregation which belong to his jurisdiction; he promulgates or causes to be promulgated the acts of the Chapter; he appoints to all the employments unreserved to the General Chapter; he distributes or approves all the obediences , revokes all those whose nomination belongs to him , and may , in cases of necessity , suspend and replace provisionally, by other religious of the same rank , even those whose nomination belongs tho the General Chapter.

58. He visits or causes to be visited, when he judges it expedient, all the establishments of the Congregation.

59. He assembles the General Chapter; he presides it , as well as all the provincial and local chapters as he likes the best.

60. The deposition of the Superior General can only be proposed to the Holy See by the

General Chapter, for irreligion, heresy, immorality, incapacity or bad administration, with the two thirds of the suffrages.

CONSTITUTION IX.

Of the Council of the Superior General.

61. The Council of the Superior General is composed of his Assistants under his presidency.

62. When it is needed, it meets at the will and after the convocation of the Superior General.

63. The Council examines the accounts which are rendered every six months by the Provincials or the Vicars respecting the temporal administration of the houses under their jurisdiction.

CONSTITUTION X.

Of the Assistants.

64. The Assistants are elected for six years by the General Chapter, among the members

having at least four years of profession, and revocable at the will of the General. They form the Council of the Superior General and act in his stead when needed; in fine they act under his absolute dependance, as being his organs, and only quit him with his consent.

CONSTITUTION XI.

Of the Procurator General.

65. The Procurator General is the representative of the whole Congregation near the Holy See; therefore he generally resides at Rome, where he may fulfil, at the same time, the functions of Provincial. He is elected by the General Chapter for six years. He acts under the direction of the Superior General.

66. He may be reelected indefinitely, but never for life. He must have four years of profession.

CONSTITUTION XII.

Of the Secretary General and of the other Secretaries.

67. The Secretary General must have been professed four years. He is intrusted, under the authority of the Superior General : 1. with the keeping of the registers and acts of the General Chapter ; 2. with the care of preparing and dispatching the correspondence non confidential of the Superior General, either with strangers, or with the different establishments of the Congregation. He is elected for six years by the General Chapter.

68. He commits to writing all the acts and reports of the general administration, excepted the reports of the Sessions of the General Chapter that selects for each its Secretary of Session.

69. He is by right a member of the General Chapter, and fulfils all the other temporary offices which are delegated by the Council of the Superior General.

70. The other Secretaries are elected at

the majority of the votes within the Chapters or Councils where they have to discharge their office, or else they are selected by their Superiors for their private administrations, but then without votes within the Councils or Chapters.

CONSTITUTION XIII.

Of the Steward General and of the other Stewards.

71. The Steward General must have four years of profession He is elected by the general Chapter for six years, and is intrusted, under the authority of the Superior General, with receiving and centralising the particular accounts of all the establishments, by the intervention of the Provincials, in order to present the half-yearly, annual and triennial summary as well as the general inventory, either to the Council of the Superior General, or in the Gencral Chapter during its Sessions.

72. The particular Stewards of each house are named by simple obedience, and they

administer the temporalities under the authority of the local Superiors. They send their accounts every quarter, to the Provincial, and through him to the Steward General, according to the mode appointed by the latter. They generally fulfil the office ot Treasurers.

CONSTITUTION XIV.

Of the Treasurer General.

73. The Treasurer General must be professed four years. He is elected for six years by the General Chapter.

74. He has the charge to collect, in the name of the Congregation, all the sums which the different establishments are bound to pay to the Mother-House. He is charged, moreover, with the remittance of all the funds which are destined to them, upon sight of the accounts and orders agreed upon by the Steward General and signed by the Superior General.

75. He keeps an exact account of the sums received and paid.

CONSTITUTION XV.

Of the Provincials.

76. The Provincials elected for six years must be professed four years at least and experienced in the functions of administration.

77. They administer their Provinces as the Superior General of the Congregation, in the limits of their jurisdiction, with the assistance of a Provincial Chapter which meets every year, and of a Council which assembles when needed.

78. The Provincial Chapter meets every year, at the Provincial House, provided the Superior General does not order otherwise with regard to time and place.

79. It is composed : of the Provincial, president, and the Superior of each House of the Province or their delegate.

80. Before their separation, the Chapter will emit a vote on the question of knowing

whether the Rules and Constitutions are observed in the Province? and in the negative case, the following question will be proposed to the Chapter : Is there any reason to beg humbly the Superior General to cause the Province to be visited?

81. All the acts of the Chapter shall be briefly transmitted to the Superior General in the ensuing fornight.

82. The Provincial Chapter receives the accounts and approves the budgets of the Establishments of the Province of which, it examines all affairs, in order to form its judgement; but it is necessary that its decisions should be approved by the Superior General to bring out their effect.

83. The Council of the Provincial is composed of his Assistant, of the Steward and of two members appointed by the Superior General, among the Professed of the Province, in observing the equality between the two classes conformably to the composition of the General Chapter.

84. The Provincial consults his Council

concerning the advice to be transmitted to the Superior General with regard to the foundation of new Houses or the suppression of Houses already founded as well as touching the punishments to be inflicted in matters of important discipline.

85. If the Provincial cannot visit himself every year, each establishment of his Province, he must send a special visitor to have an account given him, and in all the difficulties he will meet with, he will hasten to refer to the Superior General in whose dependance he must always administer, as being his representative.

86. The present Constitution will only be brought into activity when the General Chapter will have judged it opportune to demand its execution to the Holy See.

87. Provisionally the Provincials will be replaced by simple Vicars appointed by the Superior General and revocable by him *ad nutum*, to whose charge he will commit a determined number or Houses or Establishments, with attributions equally determined by him.

CONSTITUTION XVI.

Of the Superiors and Directors of particular Establishments

88 The Superiors and Directors of particular Establishments are appointed or approved by the Superior General and receive the one or the other of those two tittles according to the importance of their Houses.

89. They are taken indifferently among the Salvatorists and the Josephites.

90. The Heads of important Establishments are aided, generally, by an Assistant, a Steward and special Prefect whose obediences are approved by the Superior General, on the presenting of the Provincial.

91. The Superiors or Directors have a Council or Chapter, similar to those of the Provincials and Superior General.

92. They are under the immediate jurisdiction of the Provincial who visits them or

cause them to be visited, receives their quaterly accounts, solves the difficulties of his Province and renders an account of all to the administrators of the Mother-House.

93. The Stewards or those who act in their stead keep regular accounts which shows their receipts and expenses according to a determined mode ; they make, every six months, a general account that the Provincial approves and sends to the Steward General.

CONSTITUTION XVII.

Of the Vows.

94. In the Congregation four kinds of vows are to be distinguished, viz : the vows of Poverty, of Chastity, of Obedience and the vow of Foreign missions.

95. Those who are admitted to the profession are obliged to make the perpetual vows of Poverty, Chastity and Obedience ; those who have not the requisite age, must bind themselves by annual vows before their Su-

perior, till they attain the age to emit them definitively.

96. No one is obliged to make the vow of the Foreign missions, those who feel themselves called by God to go in whichever place of the world that the Superior General will please to send them, might make it.

97. No one can have his vows unbound save by the Holy See, and by the Superior General who unbinds the vows of Obedience and Poverty.

98. The obligation of the vows of Obedience and Poverty ceases by the sole fact of dismissal regularly pronounced.

99. The extent of the three vows of Poverty, Chastity and Obedience is determined in the following Constitutions.

CONSTITUTION XVIII.

Of the vow of Poverty.

100. As in the present time, in France, the civil law allows the Religious the right of possessing, acquiring and disposing of their

property, either by donation or by will, the Holy See is humbly entreated to allow in the Congregation that the vow of Poverty may not deprive either of the naked property, or of the right above mentioned, but only of the use.

101. Consequently in virtue of their vow, the professed are obliged in conscience and before God to make use of their property only in the absolute dependance of their Superiors, though they preserve the right of keeping that which they had previous to their profession, and of accepting that which might afterwards be granted them in any way whatever.

102. They are not allowed, either, to refuse the legacies which might be made them personally, or the inheritances which might fall to their share, because those are rights to which they cannot renounce without making an act of property. They are not, however, obliged to accept those legacies or inheritances for the Congregation, for the vow they have made cannot force them to it. But they must follow the advice of their Supe-

riors for the use it is expedient to make of that property, as well as of its revenue.

103. They may, previous to making their vows, leave all their property to their relations, even if these did not need it, but they could not do it after their vow of Poverty, without the permission of their Superiors.

104. However the Superiors will judge, in their prudence, whether they shall refuse that permission, owing to the situation of the families, or the danger of rendering themselves odious and provoking scandals.

105. The Congregation and even each particular house may possess, receive and give ; but all the property must be administered by the Chapters , Superiors, Directors, with wisdom and economy, according to determined Rules, without the administrators appropriating to themselves personally, any portion whatever.

106. The Superiors are obliged to take care that nothing be introduced into the furniture of the houses and the objects for the

use of each inmate which is not conform to religious simplicity.

107. No one has the right to make use of an object as the owner of it, nor even keep it for his own use without permission. The vow obliges, moreover, to keep oneself in the habitual disposition of renouncing to the possession and use of all the things which have been permitted, from the first moment that the Superiors order it.

CONSTITUTION XIX.

Of the vow of Chastity.

108. The vow of Chastity obliges those who make it, to renounce not only to marriage, but to all the pleasures of the flesh, forbidden by the sixth precept, and to abstain from all that is contrary to the purity of the mind and body, under pain of committing a double sin, in breaking, at the same time, the law of God and their vow.

CONSTITUTION XX.

Of the vow of Obedience.

109. The foundation of every Religious Congregation, as of all holyness, is in obedience, because in the practice of this virtue consists that perfect abnegation that Our Lord has so much recommended, saying : " If any one wishes to be my disciple, let him deny himself. "

110. By the vow of Obedience one his obliged to obey to the legitimate Superiors in all that is not contrary to the letter or spirit of the Constitutions, Rules, Decrees and Regulations of the Congregation, approved by the Chapter General.

111. Although every Superior may as well as the Superior General, give orders in virtue of holy Obedience, it is to be done but seldom, and for weighty and urgent reasons.

112. In virtue of their vow of Obedience, all are obliged to obey, 1° to the Pope, who

is the first of all their Superiors, 2° to the Ordinary in all that he has the right to command them through his Episcopal jurisdiction.

CONSTITUTION XXI.

Of the Admission to the Profession.

113. No ecclesiastical Novice will be admitted to the profession before twenty one years of age complete, and no Josephite before twenty five and the emission of the three vows of Poverty, Chastity and Obedience, at least since one year, after an examination on the knowledge appropriate to the subject, on his conduct and religious dispositions. This examination must take place two months previous to the end of the Novitiate before the council of the house which he belongs to.

114. If the vote is favourable, the President will inform the Provincial or Vicar who will provoke a final decision on the part of the Superior General. If the vote is contrary, it will belong to the Provincial or Vicar

to pronounce the dismissal or adjournment of the Novice.

CONSTITUTION XXII.

Of the Dismissal of the Professed.

115. Whoever will be regularly dismissed from the Congregation, will be, thereby, released from the vows of Obedience and Poverty, and he will be informed of it before his leaving, in mentioning it even in the act of his dismissal.

116. Now the causes of dismissal for the professed are : 1° the five primary impediments which have been spoken of in Constitution V, if they have been concealed first and happen to be discovered after the profession ; 2° the obduracy in some vice of a contumacious member who keeps no account of the penances imposed by the Superior , although the prayers of the Congregation and all the other means that prudence and charity may suggest, have been employed for his conversion.

117. But no one can be dismissed, before having taken respecting him, an information directed according to the instructions of the Superior General or the Provincial, and his dismissal can be executed but after the sentence rendered by the Superior General having the assent of the two thirds of his councillors.

CONSTITUTION XXIII.

Of the ranks and precedency of each member.

118. The ecclesiastics will be placed always and everywhere, in the assemblies of the Congregation, according to the order of hierarchy and dignity, before the Josephites, each in the following order : 1° the Superior General; 2° his Assistants, according to their elective rank; 3° the Procurator General; 4° the Secretary General; 5° the Steward General; 6° the Treasurer General; the Provincials; the members of the General Chapter; the Assistants of the Provincials; the local Superiors and their assistants; the Masters of the Novices; the Directors of the

Candidates; the Stewards of each house; all, each according to the order of foundation of their houses, and seniority of election.

119. Then will come the other members, each according to his rank of dignity or profession, of taking of the habit or entrance in the Congregation.

CONSTITUTION XXIV

Of the case of dissolution.

120. The Congregation being formed of two societies between which the Devil might attempt to sow the seeds of discord, the members of the General Chapter, Provincials, Superiors, Masters of Novices and Directors of Candidates, will be made to promiss, not only to say nothing and do nothing contrary to that union, but moreover to prevent, as much as possible, others saying or doing any thing of the like, and that under pain of being deprived of all office and dignity.

121. It is for the same purpose that it has

been enacted from the beginning, that all the property, although deriving, for the greater part, from the Salvatorists, should be laid in common; that one would avoid in the annual and general accounts to make known the income of each Society; that in the accounts of the Establishments, one would shown annually the general state of the receipts and expenses without pointing out what regards either the Salvatorists or the Josephites; in fine that should the Congregation be dissolved, all the property and produce should be handed over to the free disposal of the Holy See.

122. Besides, all the difficulties which may arise, whether they regard the temporal, or whether they relate to the spiritual things, will be irrevocably judged by the Holy See, all the members of the Congregation leaving it to its sovereign decision, whatever it may be.

CONSTITUTION XXV.

Of the teaching in the Society.

123. The teaching given by the society is of three kinds : 1° The teaching of Philosophy, Theology and the other Ecclesiastical sciences in the Seminaries; 2° the secondary teaching in the Colleges or Institutions, i.e. the Belles-Lettres, Sciences and the Arts which constitute an accomplished education; 3° In the schools the primary teaching which comprises Grammar, Mathematics, Sacred History, Profane History, Geography, the Natural Sciences, etc., especially the Christian Doctrine.

124. The general direction of the teaching is intrusted to a Prefect of the studies who frames his dispositions together with the General whose orders he takes to transmit them to the head of each establishment.

125. The teaching whether theological or

philosophical, will be especially intrusted to men known for the orthodoxy of their principles and their attachment to the Holy See.

126. There are, in each educational establishment, of whatever nature it may be, quarterly examinations on the subjects taught.

127. A special Prefect is appointed to the direction of the studies in the houses of an importance great enough to bear that organisation.

128. The greatest care will be taken that the teaching of the Belles-Lettres be predominated by the spirit of catholicism, and the most suitable manner to develop that spirit, will be selected with caution and discretion.

129. In the Orphans' Asylums and in the houses of Agriculture and of Trades, the Christian Doctrine will form the essential part of the teaching; the other sciences will remain elementary enough not to inspire young men with thought of deserting their

social situation : in the case that dispositions should be remarked; it would be judged advisable, as much as possible, to take advantage of them by peculiar means.

END.

INDEX.

www.ingramcontent.com/pod-product-compliance
Lightning Source LLC
LaVergne TN
LVHW011238110826
845150LV00006B/1676

* 9 7 8 1 4 2 5 5 1 4 0 0 6 *